CARLA A. CARLISLE
ASHLEY EILAND

Journey
to the
SON

An Unconventional Quest of Mother and Son to
Love, Light and Hope

JOURNEY TO THE SON

Self-published by Carla A. Carlisle.
Printed by Bookbaby.

This document is published by Carla A. Carlisle located in the United States of America. It is protected by the United States Copyright Act, all applicable state laws and international copyright laws. The information in this document is accurate to the best of the ability of Carla A. Carlisle at the time of writing. The content of this document is subject to change without notice.

ISBN-13: 978-1-54397-186-6 *Hardcover*

CONTENTS

PREFACE

When Carla first contacted me to write this book, I was excited, but concerned. I knew only scant pieces of her story, and even those fragments were enough to give me pause. Before this undertaking, I had never written anything so moving, so involved, or so emotionally charged. Saying "no," was never an option, but I had doubts.

A story like this requires so much trust, so much transparency, and while Carla and I had known each other for years, I wasn't sure how much she'd open up to me. I was asking to see the most painful, most hidden, and most private parts of her life--it's a lot to ask, but with every question I was blown away by her commitment to the project. At no point did Carla ever say: "that's off limits," or "I don't want to talk about that." For every one of my questions, I was given an honest, unflinching answer, and I will be forever grateful for the time we shared while writing this book.

The year I spent writing this book was perhaps some of the most grueling work I've ever done. Sitting down at my computer to type, my heart so heavy with this story, I felt it my duty to tell it correctly. I wanted the world to see Carla as I did: A brave woman facing some hard choices for a good reason. I look back now, hundreds of emails, and countless phone calls later: and I'm proud. Proud of the work we did, and proud of the story we told. Carla's "Journey to the Son" allowed me to set out on a journey of my own, and not a single part of me remains unchanged.

-Ashley Eiland

PROLOGUE

The Mother In Me

I have always wanted to be a mother.

I watched my niece and nephew grow up under the strong loving hand of my sister, reflected upon the guidance and support of my own mother and knew in my heart I wanted to be that for someone, someday. With my style, success, and a handsome husband at my side. Would I not in fact make a wonderful mother?

I knew the truth: I would.

Another truth: I couldn't.

After losing the child I was so grateful to carry, my heart began to change. Poised to join my weak and tired egg with my husband's damaged sperm in my own body, I had doubts. I thought about the babies that needed arms to hold them; and I thought of my own arms: empty, despite the money, time, and effort spent to fill them. I could be a mother, I decided, to the motherless. And though my saddened heart, betrayed by my broken body, had indeed changed, my husband's had not, and I was alone -- neither a wife nor a mother.

"Why don't you foster," my friend Claudia asked repeatedly since taking in her sister's brood to raise as her own. I eyed her messy, complicated life as one walking in the shoes of another. Could I do what she had done? Could I raise a baby I had no claim or right to? Could I fully give my love to a child that may, at any moment, be snatched from me by a system that cares more about biology than people?

I could.

I did.

My son, my sweet little boy, came into the world humbly, delivered to me in a sack full of poison by his mother, Montaya, Montaya, "MawMaw," as he would later come to call her, would for me represent everything that could be wrong with motherhood. She'll forever be the woman that gave me my child. She will forever be the woman who tried her best to take him away.

CHAPTER 1

And So It Begins

I grew up in Indiana, land of the Hoosiers, shaded by the branches of the black and white ash, in a town of about 46,000 people according to that year's census. I was born the last of two daughters to a handsome father, beautiful mother, and a sister who at four years my senior year, I found bossy but tolerable. Our home was modest, but happy, with a heavy emphasis placed on family values and responsibility. *Be sweet,* I must have heard a thousand times throughout my childhood, which I never understood. Why be sweet? I often thought to myself, when there were so many other flavors.

My parents were hardworking, quiet people who kept to themselves and liked it very much if you did the same. My father's wavy hair and my mother's light complexion drew the ire or admiration of my peers in a time when such attributes bought passage to far more privilege than it should have. My childhood, while not perfect, was charmingly benign, and in retrospect, I was blessed to grow up relatively unscathed. Never did I know the fear and uncertainty of hunger, nor did I ever fall asleep to sounds of anger between my mother and father. My sister and I grew under the steady consistent love of our parents and simply did our best to be "nice young ladies."

I remember once as a little girl, I'd been acting out in class, being silly maybe. I wasn't a bully, or even terribly disruptive, just chatty. Even then, I liked having the command of the room. I knew then that I was a person with something to say, and perhaps more importantly, I knew I was a person to whom people would listen. Eventually, my mother was called, and though she was irritated with me, she appeared more so with my teacher. "Why wouldn't you call me?" I remember her asking that teacher, her mouth a straight, unwavering line: a sure sign that she was upset "If there is *ever* a problem with *my* daughter, I need to know *before* it becomes a problem." And that was it, the only message my parents wanted to make clear to our teachers or anyone else for that matter: they were there for us. That watchful and involved spirit shaped me as a person and eventually as a mother. My parents identified issues with my sister and me and immediately sought ways to eliminate them. While we were, of course, accountable for our actions, we trusted the unwavering support and presence of our parents around every pitfall or poor choice.

I grew up in a time when women were committed to educating themselves out of the kitchen and everybody's skin color, black or white, light or dark, still mattered far too much. I began my journey within the safe, flat borders of the Midwest, where "wash" is pronounced "warsh," and Larry Bird's photo is seen as often as the president's. And though I loved my little town, for me, the only conceivable direction of my road, was "out." Being a "nice young lady" in a small pretty town, only got you so far, and I felt, in my soul, I had much farther to go.

Popular and active in school, I knew my world was bigger than the community center parking lot that so enchanted my peers. I can still feel the rumble of the asphalt as car after recklessly driven car made its way onto that asphalt drag-strip to puff and preen in front of an appreciative audience. I can see me too, head thrown back in laughter with friends, forever frozen within the glossy pages of year-book immortality.

By anyone's measure, I think I would have been considered pretty. I was tall, with an athletic build, and a youthful arrogance you could see in my stride and in the haughty flip of my hair. I was in the flag corps, got good grades, and generally passed the time the way most "cool" girls do in high school. I hung out with the 'bad boys', went on dates, did my homework, watched my sister fall in love and eventually marry the boy next door, and burned quietly knowing there was more out there for me.

As the pseudoscience of "birth order" has often suggested, as the youngest, I felt pressure early on to rebel against very nearly everything. My mother would later remark, sometimes with a smile playing on her beatific face, that I was "a handful." Both my parents worked, and as a result, I was often left in the care of my well-meaning, though insufferably responsible sister. For Patricia, the role of temporary caregiver simply meant "de facto mother," and I resented her position and power over me in the absence of our parents. It was here, in the sunny halls of our little Kokomo home, that saw the start of a rivalry, which even now, I'm not sure we've ever really been able to escape. Saintly and conservative, my sister was everything I would not allow myself to be. If she went right, I made it my mission to go left, and yet, it has always amazed me that we end up in the exact same place.

My sister and I, though different in so many ways, were not only fortunate but blessed to have parents that invested and believed in our education. When the time finally came to leave and make something of ourselves, we went. My journey took me a hundred miles from home to Indiana University, Bloomington, where I earned a degree in sociology with a certificate in public affairs. During this time I also affiliated myself with Alpha Kappa Alpha Sorority, Inc. and drew an incredible source of strength from the women around me -- my sorors. Effortlessly beautiful, successful, and powerful, AKA's, for me, were representative of everything I knew I wanted to be. Swathed in the Salmon Pink and Apple Green of my sisters, I felt the strength and wisdom of the women before me and made it my goal to earn the benefit of their legacy.

From those humble Hoosier halls, my drive and ambition took me to Washington D.C. where I worked as an investigative specialist for the FBI and as a personnel security specialist for the United States Senate. I later found myself an alumna of both The American University and The John Hopkins University, earning graduate degrees and opening doors I'd only glimpsed from the concrete steps of my A-frame childhood home.

Though I followed my sister to Washington, our lives diverged entirely. While she found success in marriage, work, and motherhood, I bucked those conventions and lived my life as fabulously as I could.

I earned a reputation as a "party girl," though without the destructive habits such a moniker might suggest. I was, at all times, in control of myself, but I did love to be a part of the action. If there was a place to be, I'd be there. I would show up with my girls, dressed to the nines, my long neck thrown back in amusement as the men around me did their best to take me home.

My life was an exotic array of clubs, parties, restaurants, and within the swirl of its colors and flavors, I was living the life I'd always dreamed I would. With so many distractions: names, business cards, and numbers, I had a rich and varied romantic life. It was during this time I made the acquaintance of a young, handsome football player and fell in love. He played for the Washington Redskins, and side by side, we were the picture of everything I had ever hoped to achieve: we were young, black, and extraordinary.

I loved that man, and though he was plagued by more demons than I could reasonably be expected to fight, I stayed. I think here began a pattern that would haunt me my whole life: the need to fix what was broken in others. As a strong, successful woman, I rarely sought my equal in a partner, focusing instead on men I would need to *bring up* to my level. Though outwardly, yes, as an NFL football player my lover had achieved much in his own right, inwardly, he was a mess. Like most young black athletes, he knew how to spend, but didn't know how to save, and he wore his money draped about his shoulders like a security blanket; hiding a small, scared child beneath it.

Off and on, we were together for ten years. We tried and tried to start a family. What perfect babies we would make, I thought to myself with each disappointing arrival of my period. I think it was during this time, the first seeds of worry were sown and I began to wonder if something might be wrong with me. In the meantime, I waited. I waited to get pregnant, waited for him to grow up, get clean, knock-up women that weren't me, and then eventually, I couldn't bear to wait any longer, and I was running out of time to waste. I said goodbye to the life we should have had, and left him behind.

CHAPTER 2
Failure & Loss

I had achieved nearly everything I'd ever wanted. Professionally, I was a force to be reckoned with within my field, and people up and down the ladder knew my name. The pressure to be elegant, but appropriate, strong, but not aggressive, feminine, but not weak, was a balancing act I executed with aplomb, and I strode the halls of my office in my tailored suits and tasteful, workplace heels, with the confidence of one who'd earned the right to be there. If I wanted anything, be it professionally or personally, I knew I had the means to get it. Failure had never been, nor would it ever be an option for me.

All my life, I had been driven by a need to carve out a place for myself at the top of the world. There was no position out of reach of my long, capable arms, and if confronted by a shelf too high, I grew the required height to put it firmly within my reach. I went up the ladder, rung by rung, level by level, simply because that's what life had been for me: a series of vertical moves. The top is where I'd always felt most comfortable, but for all my success, I knew that while I might have had ambition, I had lacked purpose.

Being a mother, warming bottles, kissing boo-boos, I felt these things would give me that purpose. My life didn't feel empty. I didn't want a baby to fill what was missing, I wanted a baby to share in what was present. My efforts to conquer the known world needed a beneficiary, a vessel into which I could place all my good intentions. What was the use of all my success, advice, experiences, and love, if I couldn't pass it on or put it somewhere meaningful?

As a single, successful black woman, I relished the financial and sexual freedom this position brought me. I'd spent my twenties and thirties in a whirl of parties, short skirts, and colorful drinks, each experience blending into the next like a vivid watercolor painting entitled, "Fun."

As I neared my forties, the steady drum of motherhood began to beat beneath the surface of my existence with increasing speed and intensity. I had a box of glossy pictures to pull out and sift through, to show the world I had been there and I had had a great time. But -- and this is the question that most often haunted me late at night alone in my bed --when I put the box away, what was left?

When I met Brian, the drumbeat that so moved me grew louder and louder. Its crashing rhythm drowned out my common sense, my better judgment, and soon I was consumed by its music. I wanted to have a baby, and in my mind, the means by which this goal was accomplished didn't matter much. We met, I beguiled him with my spaghetti casserole (one of the very few things I could make in the kitchen), and within six months, we were married.

I may have made a mistake.

It really didn't take long for the marriage to fall apart. Looking back, I have to wonder if, at any point, we were married at all. Joined together in the name of matrimony? Yes. True partners for better or worse, equally yoked? Never. I remember our wedding on the sun-soaked beaches of Barbados. We looked so beautiful there against the reddening sky, unsure or in denial of the miseries just around the corner. I remember sliding the key into the lock of our first house together, which no amount of effort, furniture, or love could ever turn into a home.

In addition to our fertility issues, there were just so many other challenges on which to focus; financial issues, for instance. Brian was broke, and our lifestyle was subsidized in large part by me and my efforts. We also had intimacy issues. For all his handsomeness and gym-toned physique, Brian was a terrible lover. Never have I been so holistically dissatisfied in a relationship. Perhaps to add insult to injury, it quickly became clear Brian was a chronic adulterer, as well. He seemed to cheat with an aimlessness that focused on quantity over quality. By the end of my marriage, the failure to start a family seemed almost comically small against the backdrop of so many other disappointments.

When I met him, the same girlish fantasies that take ahold of all women soon took over me. He was beautiful and so wonderfully kind to not only his mother and the other women in his life, but to the women in mine, as well. The way he doted on my mother and sister, tended to my mother when she was ill, worked, I think now, as a type of magic trick, making me focus on the shiny ball in one hand while ignoring the mischief of the other.

To fully cement my enchantment, Brian worked with emotionally disturbed children and wanted badly himself to be a father. In the beginning, it seemed as if he were crafted by every dream and desire I had ever held in regard to an "ideal" mate. Never had I met a man more adoring and more attentive than my Brian. He seemed to worship the very ground I walked on, and after so many years of having my temple destroyed and disrespected, did I not deserve a little praise?

Our mutual desire to begin a family expedited our brief courtship, and we began our journey to parenthood with a frightening speed and intensity. Now in my 40s, I no longer had the luxury of time and set about funneling my energies and resources into producing the outcome I wanted most: pregnancy.

I have always been a data-driven person. Numbers, charts, information I could plot on a graph, had always been comforting to me. There was safety and surety in logic, and this was no less true on my path to a positive pregnancy test. Because I knew the risks and struggles associated with an over 40 pregnancy, our journey truly began in the clinic, not in the bedroom. Perhaps there's something to be said about the clinical, utterly unromantic way we were forced to go about things, but I could leave nothing to chance.

The news, as I had long suspected, was not good. I had suffered from fibroids, a condition which causes the growth of tumors in the reproductive system, for most of my adulthood, and the resulting surgery had indeed taken a toll on my fertility. To dig the knife ever so much deeper, it appeared my strong, beautiful husband had fertility issues of his own. Hiding within the comfort of his assumed virility, low sperm count coupled with low sperm motility, dashed our hopes of conception even further. It appeared that his chiseled physique and ample biceps had not been achieved without aid. After a lengthy Q&A with our specialist, it came to light that Brian had been juicing for quite some time, and I, his bride of less than one year, never knew. His prolonged steroid use, which had carved him into the perfect man, ironically, had robbed him of the ability to be one. We were two halves of one broken whole. Perhaps there is something to be said of that as well.

I don't think anyone can ever really prepare you for the devastation of infertility. The loneliness, the shame, the endless well-meaning platitudes from women whose homes and social media accounts are filled with the sticky, gap-toothed grins of their offspring. Every period you welcomed in relief, every birth control pill taken to stave off the future you'd never have any way comes back to mock you when you're feeling at your lowest. You question every fertile year you casually squandered and a crushing insecurity overtakes you. There is no emptier feeling than "barren," and though I had a man at my side, the failure in that diagnosis was all mine.

The state of Maryland, where we were living at the time, had large incentives that went toward aiding struggling couples on the quest to conception, and from there we stumbled confidently toward three letters so common on this journey: IVF.

From the start, Brian began to pull away. Though he wanted to be a father just as badly as I wanted to be a mother, he became increasingly distant during the process. I felt more and more alone, and our marriage became more and more strained. I don't know if it was the stress of what we were going through, his feelings of guilt, or the incessant chime of his phone that took his focus away from me and the life we struggled in vain to create. It took so little time for Brian's extramarital dalliances to interfere in our marriage. It became clear to me that these women had always been a part of our relationship. For all the humiliation and anger I endured with each found text, email, and receipt, one thought remained fixed: he was my husband, and we were going to have a baby.

The entire process was both tedious and without joy. Any hope of conceiving "the old-fashioned way," was minuscule, and so we strove to make a baby through the expensive miracle of science. The hormone injections, constant visits to the clinic, and the uncomfortable egg retrieval process, in which a thin needle was inserted through my vagina were, I felt, small prices to pay for the chance to have a baby. I would have done anything.

Though Brian declined to accompany me to our appointment, the transfer of five embryos into my uterus yielded one attachment, and against all odds: I was pregnant. I finally had everything I had ever wanted: A husband, a marriage, and now, a baby.

Due to its high-risk nature, my pregnancy was treated with the utmost delicacy. During this time, my husband returned to the sweet, attentive man I'd fallen for, and my temple flourished under his adoration. I felt our baby growing inside me and I could not remember a time when I was happier. The Lord had listened, and he had answered, and I was grateful.

As part of my treatment, I was due to have a vaginal sonogram every week. While the slick, cold probe of the machine wasn't thrilling, I saw it as a special time with my baby. Every week I had tangible, living proof of my diligence and faithfulness. For six visits, I marveled at the changes my little miracle underwent, and I fantasized about the brilliant, beautiful, happy child he or she would later become. For six visits, I had hope. On the seventh, I lost it all.

No heartbeat, the doctor told me. While the news was no doubt common, over 30% of women over the age of 40 suffered miscarriages through the IVF process, it shattered something within me, and I was never again the same. I carried on another week before passing the embryo, sac and all, from my body, and I stood empty: a failure. I had failed as a woman and as a wife, and in the midst of that failing, I barely knew myself.

Our marriage in shambles, we halted the second round of IVF and moved to North Carolina for a fresh start. The vibrant green landscape, alongside buildings of glittering steel and glass, seemed like the perfect place for a fresh perspective, and I was excited to begin again. We had been through so much our first year together: a hasty marriage, numerous infidelities, fertility issues, and the loss of a child; it seemed not only necessary but vital to any success we might one day enjoy, that we leave our life in Maryland and its many small tragedies behind.

Though I did not care for our new fertility specialists--I found them to be both insensitive and unprofessional -- we trudged toward another round of IVF. Without the incentives we enjoyed in Maryland, the full cost of treatment fell heavily on our shoulders, and we knew it was our last chance. The odds of success were even lower now that Brian's sperm had lost all motility and we waited, without much enthusiasm, for the news we already knew in our hearts: it was over.

So we fought. We fought because he spent thousands upon thousands of dollars of my money. Suits, alcohol, electronics, whatever flashed, beeped, or glittered, ended up as line items on my credit card bill. We fought because it seemed not to matter where we lived, women that looked nothing like me continued to turn his head, and fill his inbox. We fought because it was all wrong, and nothing we did or tried seemed to make it right.

Near the end, we decided to enlist the services of an egg donor, and the one we found was perfect. Her genetic background was without mental or physical blemish and we both felt confident in moving forward. Against all medical advice, Brian still wanted his useless sperm to aid in fertilization. Although I felt this to be both wasteful and arrogant, I agreed.

In the swirling storm of our continued struggles, Brian's mother became ill, and though he tried to get back to Maryland in time to see her, she passed away. Putting our new plans for a baby on pause, I went to join my husband in support, not knowing that I'd soon return to North Carolina alone.

I arrived in Maryland to find my husband much changed. I was greeted by a man that did not seem to need or want my love and support. And I did still love him. Through everything, I loved him and held fiercely to that love. I saw what we could be together, and I saw success in a future for which we'd already sacrificed so much. I remembered the man who, not so long ago, had rubbed my feet and brought me flowers. I loved the man... I still wanted to be the father of my children, but could not understand why he would barely look at me and refused me a place in his mother's home after her funeral. I chalked it up to grief. Surely the death of his mother had taken a toll on him and he was acting out. Keeping my stance firm, I insisted on being by his side whether he wanted me there or not. What kind of wife would I be if I let him suffer alone?

After the funeral, when the food had been eaten and the condolences given, things had not returned to normal. Late into the night, I lay next to him, awake, upset about his demeanor and behavior towards me since my arrival and waited for understanding and clarity. I worried and prayed, only to have my thoughts cleaved by the metallic chirping of a phone. Its muted, but no less shrill notifications, moved me from the bed in search of its origin, the unease in my stomach rivaling the numbness I felt elsewhere.

I ended up in the kitchen. Dark and cold after such a sad event, my disquiet deepened, and I waited. The interfering *buzz* led me to a drawer, but I paused before opening it. Who would be calling so late? I wondered. I reached out my hand, hooking my fingers, ready to pull it open and draw out its noisy contents, but I didn't want to. I knew once I opened this drawer, I could never shut it again.

I slid it open carefully, not wanting to wake anyone. It held the normal contents of a kitchen drawer: papers, toothpicks, and hundreds of ketchup packets. Among the detritus was a slim, black flip-phone: one I immediately recognized as his mother's. With shaking hands I picked it up, opening it with a *snap!* and gasped without surprise at the frequency and volume of texts all intended, it seemed, for my husband.

I miss you, baby.

I wore black today in honor of your mother.

I wish I had been there to hold your hand.

I love you.

I felt more exhausted than angry. I stood there, in my husband's dead mother's kitchen, after supporting him through a funeral he had the audacity to pay for with my credit card, while another woman waited for him to say he loved her back. With my back to the kitchen counter, my heart on the cold kitchen floor, I wondered just how hard was it supposed to be.

I confronted him. He asked for a divorce. We drove back to North Carolina in a heavy silence punctuated by anger and hurt. We made love, he left and never came back.

If I really took the time to tally up my losses, I'm not sure it'd be fair to count Brian as one among them. He had never been the right choice, and no baby we might have conceived or devised would have been enough to make that fact otherwise.

CHAPTER 3

God's Gift and Her

My wounds thoroughly licked, I set about doing what I did best: I identified problems and executed solutions, just as my parents had done with my sister and me. My inability to conceive a child didn't remove me from the race, and I set my sights on a different goal.

I was skeptical at first. Could I really be a foster mother? I thought of all the things that could go wrong, and I thought of all the issues for which I just did not feel prepared. I'd be bringing a child into my home, yes, but also their history, their experiences, and a number of other unknown variables. I was excited, but a part of me was scared. But, in the face of that fear, I couldn't have asked for a better support system in North Carolina. Patricia, the sister from whom I'd tried so hard to distinguish myself, had also found her way to "The Tar Heel State" for work, and a number of girlfriends, work colleagues, and sorors were present to help me through a challenging transition of not only thought but action.

When the call came, I wasn't ready. A little boy, born prematurely, in need of a home. A baby. A sweet little boy for me to love. I just knew, before I ever even met him, that he was my answered prayer.

17

Though adopting through the foster care system was difficult in the state of North Carolina, I was told the probability of adopting Devon was high. When he was born, traces of cocaine were found in his meconium stool and he was immediately taken away, safe from a mother that would rather see her baby sick than quell her own addiction to destruction.

In situations like these, I was told, separating the child from the toxic influence of the mother was the first order of business. Due to the high-risk nature and lifestyle of his mother, Devon was born two months premature and immediately processed into the system. He came into my life about ten days later.

When I first expressed an interest in fostering, my hope had been for an older child. I saw the need for so many children, past the age of "precious," to be brought into safe, loving homes, and I felt I could do that. However, the process soon proved to be overwhelming. I was presented with a number of children from ages three to five but found it difficult to make a decision. How could I choose one need over another when I knew I couldn't take them all? What made one child more worthy of my love than another, and furthermore, who was I to decide such a thing? When I got the call for Devon, my prayers were answered, it seemed, but not in the way I expected. Instead of having to be the one to choose, I was chosen.

Though born prematurely, Devon was still a big baby. At over five pounds, his appetite for life, and love, and formula was large, and I delighted in feeding each physical and emotional need. It seemed as though God himself, gave me the baby I wasn't able to have, and I was enchanted by him at once. The minute I saw those eyes, so big and so open, watchful--I knew we belonged to each other. I was no less captivated by his ten beautiful toes, long fingers, and soft brown face because he came from someone else's womb. The moment I saw him look at me, I was his mother.

In the state of North Carolina, reunification, above all other solutions, is the chief objective when it comes to child welfare services. Giving families the tools to be successful and stay together is, of course, a noble concern, but not always achievable. In Devon's case, reunification seemed unlikely as he was taken away from her at birth. I was told that 99% of children taken from their mothers that early did not go back. Upon his birth, Montaya declined to name a father on his birth certificate, and so he became, at a few hours old, a ward of the state, in need of a home.

If you asked me what it was like to hold him for the first time, what could I tell you? How do you describe the first breath of air you ever took? Though vital and necessary an event it was, it was what you were always meant to do. Never had anything in my whole life leading up to that moment felt so right. I had been waiting for him for so long. When my heart found my way to him, that was it, I was breathing.

There were, of course, concerns. Children born to drug users were often diagnosed with a number of physical, emotional, and behavioral maladies down the road. Issues with self-regulation, aggression, and cognitive processing (drugabuse.gov) were all future factors to consider, but it didn't matter. I finally had my baby, and he was perfect.

While I wasn't remotely familiar with any of it, I had made myself ready. When Devon and I became a family, it wasn't without help. I had an arsenal of nannies, night nurses, family, and friends to navigate the choppy waters of "mommy-hood." Like any mother, I was bewitched by every coo, spit up, and poopy my son made. Though granted, this was not my chosen path, it now seemed the only place I was ever meant to be. I briefly gave a thought to my failed marriage and my desperate efforts and concessions to make the perfect family and marveled at how life had so curiously conspired to grant me exactly that. I was exhausted but happy. Perhaps the only wrinkle in the colorful tapestry of my new life was the *business* of becoming a mother.

It has always struck me as both hilarious and ironic the only thing needed as proof of your fitness to *be* a parent, is to *have* a child. There are no court officials sending you letters demanding that you study up for your new role, no visits from social workers, no meetings to challenge your abilities as a future mother or father. No, if you could *have* a baby, then you *deserved* a baby, with so many children…..beyond, I wondered: *How could that be true?*

While new mothers the world over cradled their newborns in their arms and grappled with the holistic fearfulness of keeping such a small, precious thing unbroken, I had CFT: Child and Family Team Meetings, and it's here that I met Montaya for the first time.

CFT meetings are chiefly designed to be a platform for discussion about the best interests of the child. Plans are put into place for intervention, family needs, permanence, and counseling for the continued health of both the child and the birth family. As Devon's possible "forever home," it was vital that both I and his birth mother be in attendance.

To that end, it was a bumpy, not at all very punctual road to my first meeting with Montaya. CFT meetings must happen within a certain number of days after the child is taken from the birth mother, and in typical Montaya fashion (I was soon to learn), she was over two hours late to our first meeting. The woman with whom I would eventually share the title of "mother," strode in like a queen with the man assumed to be Devon's father. Trailing the end of that sad processional was a grown daughter she'd previously lost custody of and that now-grown daughter's fiancé.

We appraised each other coolly, each of us desperately mining out the value of the other across the long expanse of a cheap, wood-laminate conference table. With a bevy of social workers and counselors, the scene seemed more appropriate for a hostage negotiation. It didn't take long for it to feel that way as well.

"So this her?" She spoke around me, jerking a defiant, dismissive chin in my direction.

"I'm Carla," I broached, prepared to make nice for the sake of my son. If not for her, this woman who couldn't quite meet my eyes, Devon wouldn't be here. That small fact alone was worth something, if not everything to me, and it was a fact, that for the next several years, she would not let me forget.

She quickly cut her eyes to her companions when I spoke, a glint of mocking lurking there. That was all right, I decided. I had my own assessments to make.

She was a woman of considerable weight and charisma. I could tell she was used to the attention she generated, her eyes flitting to every face in the room. She'd thrown together an outfit, I assumed, that was meant to look professional: a tight black t-shirt, the v of which displayed breasts that would never feed her child, and gray slacks, pilling at the thigh, probably worn thin from shuffling to and from meetings such as this. I looked for my son in her face, this woman separated from me by so many choices and experiences but bound to me by one. I looked hard and saw him everywhere. I saw him in her large, expressive eyes, the lids hooded and sleepy. I noticed she had a small metal stud through her eyebrow, through skin the same flawless cocoa I so lovingly bathed every night, and I felt myself soften when his round little cheeks peeked from the edges of her smile. This was the tough leather hide from which my baby was cut, how bad could she be?

I couldn't make much of the other two with her. The daughter looked like a smaller, less confident version of Montaya, and as such, was very easy to forget. While Montaya's eyes were bright and energetic, her daughter's bore the haunted look of a person waiting to be hammered down if they even dared to stand up. Wayne, Montaya's boyfriend, was wholly unremarkable. The definition of shifty, he seemed constantly to be in agitated motion. Fingers, ashy at the knuckle, weaving themselves into knot after knot, feet tapping, eyes darting every so often to the door; Wayne looked like a man who always yearned to be somewhere else. Even though Montaya had neglected to put his name on Devon's birth-certificate, I'm not sure it would have mattered. If my son's resemblance to his mother was an echo, then his resemblance to his father was a shout.

"First of all," Montaya cut through the chatter like a laser. Everyone, myself included, quieted their discussion at the sound of her voice. DSS may have called the meeting, but there was no mistake to be made about who was running it. "I don't want her," she pointed a bone straight, accusatory finger at her daughter, "to come nowhere near my baby."

Her daughter, Tonya, rolled her eyes but stayed silent. The animosity between them was clear, but not my business. I looked at the sea of faces around the table, waiting patiently for the meeting's focus to return to my son.

"Montaya," the social worker assigned to Devon's case chimed in, "we're all here to figure out what's best for Devon at this time," she spoke in the soft soothing tones of a person used to de-escalating volatile situations, and I was grateful for her presence. I had never been around people so prone to discord and destruction; unaware that I, too, would soon become an expert in de-escalation.

"Just make sure she don't get my baby," Montaya humphed one last time before crossing her arms and leaning back in her chair, springs creaking loudly in the following silence. Later in our relationship, Montaya would make it known to me that Tonya, the daughter for whom she had so much contempt, had slept with her own biological father in an effort to get back at her mother. What baffled me, upon hearing this story, was the placement of Montaya 's outrage. She wasn't mad at the father of her child for sleeping with his own daughter, or the obvious abuse that such an act suggested, but rather, she was upset that Tonya had the gumption to sleep with "her man." I was blown away by the implications present there, and really didn't know how to process that level of dysfunction. I instead prayed fervently for the safety and mental well-being of my son. Montaya's hatred for the young girl hung like cobwebs around the small conference room, and it was clear she wanted Devon to have nothing at all to do with her, and on that point, we quite mutually agreed.

"I gotta job," Tonya broke in fiercely, but quietly. "This man down the street say he can pay me a couple hundred dollars under the table each week, and me and my boyfriend looking at a house, so I could take him." She managed to say her piece without making eye contact with anyone. "He should stay with family," she said this last part almost to herself.

"Well in reviewing the paperwork," the social worker moved on delicately, stepping in to cut-off Montaya's no doubt colorful rebuttal to such a proposition. "That's certainly an option to leave on the table," she continued deftly, "but we're here merely to spark a *discussion* about custody, no definite decisions will be made during this session. However, we would like to come up with a feasible visitation schedule while we're all here." She looked at Tonya and Montaya with sympathetic finality, and I did feel a small measure of relief. Though all I'd been told suggested that Devon would almost assuredly not go back to his birth parents, the idea still lurked like a boogeyman beneath the covers of my mind.

Ultimately, it was decided that I would be Devon's guardian, his "foster mother," though, to me, Devon's adoption into my home and family was only a matter of time.

CHAPTER 4

Parenting 101

Two weeks into my tenure as a new mommy, a position I fell into with great ease, the few remaining specters of my past rose up in a united effort to usurp the peace and joy I'd struggled to create.

Two weeks after bringing my son home from the hospital, my doctor ordered a hysterectomy, and it was difficult to view those two events as unrelated. I had fought so long to reap a harvest from the barren field of my body, I was at odds to see it all so suddenly ended. I watched every dream I planted in my own soil grow black and die on the vine and ripped out weed after weed with tired, aching hands. In the arrival of my baby, I felt a slow rising freedom in razing that field; a field from which only misery had ever grown. With great skill and care, my surgeon excised the source of so much suffering, and in its removal, I could feel only relief. It was a door I could firmly and finally close.

Never would a baby grow in my womb, and though the reality never ceased to sting, I could lay flowers at the grave of that dream without remorse. I was single, but that was okay too. I was just fine without Brian, as this journey had always been mine to make alone, and my heart, now filled with more love than I could have ever imagined, hadn't the faintest notion of regret.

During my convalescence, I could not, and therefore did not focus on what I'd lost. Through prayer and the support of my mother, sister, and friends, I focused on the strength necessary to get back to my child. Forgotten were the babies that would never stretch and ripple the taught plains of my belly, I cared only for the one that had grown in my heart. How could I ever weep for the shortcomings of my past, when my future and all its glorious potential slept peacefully in the crib at my side?

Those first few months, Devon presented with a number of lessons learned and challenges overcome as I worked to create a life that worked for our little family. Initially, I'd brought in my mother from Indiana to help. I was wary of strangers and valued her gentleness and kind spirit, especially during my recovery. Well into her sixties, my niece and nephew now adults in their own right, my mother reprised her role as "new gramma" with a deftness and skill I found remarkable. From the moment she laid eyes on him, Devon was her grandson, and she was his "Gram." I will be forever grateful to my mother for accepting Devon outright. To her, he wasn't some defective product I had wrongfully picked up from the store and could, therefore, return with the presentation of a receipt. For her, he was and had always been, a part of our family.

In the weeks and months that followed her departure, I struggled, as many new mothers do, to find that same sense of safety and security after returning to work. I couldn't just leave him with *anyone*, and though I was reluctant, my time at home was up, and the office needed me.

Daycare was a disaster. It took no longer than a week for Devon to get sick, and I felt deep frustration with the entire process. I now had this baby, this child I so desperately wanted, and I couldn't even keep him safe from a cold? Absurd.

The Lord, however, watches us and gives us what we need. I believe that. Through a bit of inquiry, I found that my company offered up to 20 days of in-home care for infants, and just like that, Devon had a nanny. And though I knew him to be safe, warm, well-fed, and happy, I worried all the same. I worried for him when I wasn't there to do it myself, as if my presence alone guaranteed him safe passage through the snake-infested waters of this world.

But with time, little by little, I began to relax, began to settle into the role, and perhaps most essential, I began to trust. I started to trust not only myself but in the surety of the situation, as well. I really was a mother, and I really had a son. Just to say it out loud filled me with colors and sensations I'd only glimpsed from the benches of infertility. In my heart, I knew if motherhood was something I truly meant to achieve, then I would, but there had always been that quiet nagging fear in the back of my mind that said: *Yeah, but you might not.*

But now, as I pulled up picture after picture of him sleeping, him smiling, him doing anything, on my phone the same way all other mothers did, I trusted the happiness I felt, and after a while, we were okay. We were any other family.

CHAPTER 5

A Different World

"You gay?" Montaya asked me rather bluntly a few weeks after our initial meeting. In compliance with the courts, I was faithful to the weekly supervised visits between Devon and his birth family, and as a result, I had come into more contact with them than I cared for. Today we were at DSS, chatting, watching Devon be adorable together, so her question and its inappropriate nature caught me off guard.

"Excuse me?" I wasn't upset, just taken aback by such a bold inquiry into my sexuality.

"You and that nanny," she replied, swirling her hand in a vague motion, attempting to come up with a name for my supposed lover. "Y'all two are so close," she continued, saying the word *close* suggestively, "and you ain't got no man far as I can tell. You so pretty, I just figured you was a dyke." On the word, "dyke" she settled herself back against the wooden frame of the chair, a satisfied *creak* punctuating the impromptu interview.

"Well," I pressed forward gently, not sure why we were having this discussion in the first place, "I'm not gay, Montaya." I paused to pick Devon up from his car seat where he'd been propped, watching his two moms struggle to find an authentic connection. "Janet and I have formed a bond over this little one." I lifted him above my face, smiling up into his big watchful eyes. I tried to keep my tone bright and happy, free of the tension I suddenly felt at her question. I read that babies could detect negativity and didn't want to bring that into his space. "And as for the other question," I puffed my cheeks and made a silly face in response to his smile, "I like to keep my private life, private."

"Hunh," she grunted, watching me play with her son. Wayne think you real cute. He say he'll take a run at you if you get too lonely in that big ol' house of yours." She lifted her eyebrows as if offering me the deal of a lifetime, a half-smile shimmering on the edge of her cheeks.

I looked at her directly, wanting to really establish a connection so my words could neither be mistaken nor misunderstood. "Montaya," I said sweetly, "I would rather cut off both my arms and both my legs with a butcher knife before I would ever let that man touch me." The smile plastered there for Devon 's sake never left my lips. In response, Montaya threw back her head and laughed.

I looked at her then. During our time together, my focus was so fully on Devon, I never paid much attention to the tragic woman that bore him. She had, to me, the sad appearance of a circus clown after hours: wig askew, painted smile smeared around the edges of a scowl, tears staining her skin under the greasepaint. I would never condescend to feel sorry for her. Montaya had always struck me as a woman who found no value in pity. The things she told me, horrific stories of abuse and neglect, only deepened the gratitude I had toward my own parents and reinforced the notion that my Devon would never know the horrors his mother had endured.

I drew my son a bit closer to me during these talks. Our time together centered around the love we shared for our boy, but more often than not, our conversations lapsed into these unpleasant interviews and reveries. I tried my hardest never to judge a book by its cover. Trite and overused as it may be, I learned early on that just about anyone can surprise you. But in the relatively short amount of time I'd known Montaya, I'd done more than simply glance the cracked and blistered cover of her book; I'd picked her up, read the synopsis, and rifled through her wrinkled pages. Her story was tragic, yes, but beyond the narrative of abuse, I could very clearly see the subplot of illness (both mental and physical), and a cunning narcissism that demanded to be the star of every story around her, as well.

Though statistics were still on my side, *99% of children taken from the mother at birth don't go back*, I felt ill at ease in her presence, and prayed for a day when I'd no longer have to share him.

CHAPTER 6

Letting Go

Since Devon had come into my life, I was amazed at the sheer number of things there were to do in any given day. Midnight feedings, dirty diapers, the random soulful cry for no reason--all of it, every exhausting moment coupled with my continuing duties at work, made for a life I found busy but complete.

My struggles to conceive a "child of my own" and the heartache at my inability to do so seemed so far from this moment in my life. When I held my son in my arms at night and rocked him into the land of sweet dreams and teddy bears, I thanked God that he choosing me, for seeing in me a mother to this child. I thought briefly of the husband that should have been here with me and waited to feel the sting of his absence. I wondered if he'd found a woman that could bear his children, if they were happy, and if he ever thought of me.

Once, maybe a year after I brought Devon home and the war for his well-being began in earnest, Brian showed up full of good intentions and "baby I'm sorries." I invited him out to eat with Devon, "the parents," and myself to give him an idea of the reality he was trying to sweet talk himself back into.

Needless to say, an hour or two in their company prompted him to suggest "just paying them off and getting rid of them for good." I let him know in no uncertain terms that was something I simply wasn't willing to do, and it would be wise to never bring it up to me again. I now shrug uneasily at the memory. Such a Brian thing to do: buy me a present with my own money.

Tucking Devon into his crib, resting my hand on his soft, round belly, I let my mind slide back to the choices that led me here. My wish to be a mother had simmered quietly for years beneath the surface of my fierce professionalism and expensive haircuts. When I'd initially expressed an interest in motherhood, it was met with heavy skepticism. My reputation as a workaholic party-girl overshadowed the maternal urges I felt deep within me. I reflected on the past six months, one hundred and eighty days of the purest joy I had ever known. I awoke each day exhausted, anxious, and exalted. I awoke each day happy, blessed, and thrilled to be what I feared I never could be. The anguish I'd suffered in the wake of my own unmet expectations ceased to bear fruit, and in its place, wholeness bloomed like flowers from the prickly flesh of a cactus.

So the day they came and took him seemed wholly unremarkable when viewed next to the vibrant activity of so many wonderful days.

I simply woke up, and some hours into my morning, a phone call came and took my child away from me.

Drugs only found in his stool... error... reunification... today... I heard the words, registered the disembodied voice as an agent of DSS, but couldn't imagine the words to be true. Return him? To whom, how? I was his mother. He was already home. What could they possibly mean? "I don't understand," I stammered, fear making my voice small and tight.

"*Ma'am*," the caller returned, managing to sound both impatient and sorry at the same time, "*We are coming to pick up the child this evening and return him to his birth parents. The judge has ruled in favor of the birth parents, as he should have never been taken in the first place.*"

"How could that be? Drugs were found in his system!"

"*No ma'am*," the caller gently chided. "*Drugs were found in his meconium stool. The judge feels these are insufficient grounds for removal. The child will be returned today.*"

I was blindsided, caught totally off guard and totally unaware. This fear, this thing I wouldn't completely let myself believe in, had been lying in wait, watching me become comfortable, watching me fall more and more in love with my son, before opening its jaws and devouring me whole. I never even had a chance to fight.

No words, no breath, no pulse. I was made of nothing and that nothing filled me completely. The darkest corners of my soul had opened, and in a torrent of immeasurable sadness, out came everything I had ever feared.

I was not his mother.

I was not worthy to be his mother.

I did not deserve to be a mother.

And so I left work. I got into my car. And I drove to pick up my baby for the last time.

All-in-all, I gathered five trash bags. Five neatly packed trash bags to hand over to a family that, even as I sat there, had not the resources to care for the child they felt no remorse in taking from me. Five trash bags, straining, bulging with the love, it now seemed, I was no longer allowed to give him.

I was dying.

I handed over my baby, my miracle, my joy, my child to DSS and watched them drive him away.

I called my sister. I sat on my couch and I cried, alone.

Arms as empty as my heart.

I was useless. I couldn't eat, sleep, or work, and in a true moment of grace, my boss gave me leave so I could grieve the loss of my child appropriately.

During this time I tried in vain to fight, to argue, to explain the mistake they were making. Of course drugs were only found in his stool! Montaya had been in the hospital for months leading up to Devon's birth, it's probably the cleanest she'd been in years. But *99% of children taken from their mother's at birth don't go back.* The words swirled around me, their comfort merely a ruse. It was a lie.

"Cheer up!" People said to me, I suspect in an effort to seem helpful, friendly. "Cheer up! You can always try again, get another one!" In retrospect, I realize that my family and friends were only trying to help heal the wound that had opened up in the middle of my life, but to suggest that I could simply replace my child seemed such a thoughtless cruelty to me. I could no more "shake it off" and "move on" any more than a birth mother could have. During this time, I came to recognize that even though I felt like any other mother, I was not any other mother in the eyes of those closest to me and in the eyes of society.

I had no right, it seemed, to grieve. In anguish, I struggled to reach out, to lean on my girlfriends for support, but time and again the message I received was: *let it go; move on.* Devon was no more than a puppy I'd taken in and loved and fed, and for whom I'd put newspaper out on the floor until the rightful owners came with their relieved "thank you" to whisk him away to his actual home. The bond I felt with him was seemingly fiction, a fabrication of my desperate soul, and really why should I cry? He was never really mine, right?

And though I learned to shutter my pain against the unsought opinions of my peers and family, his cries kept me awake at night. Was he looking for me, I wondered? Where was he? Did he have enough? Enough food, enough love, enough warmth, enough anything? The weeks after his departure were perhaps some of the darkest I'd ever known, and I felt certain I would not survive them. My child was in danger, and a technicality kept me tethered to my cave; a dragon without teeth. I walked past his room, saw debris from the life I almost had and tried so hard not to disappear.

But as I said, the Lord listens. He listens for what we are afraid to wish for. He searches the silence within us to give us what we need. And just as a phone call took him away. A phone call brought him back to me.

Her number sat, unsent, in the electric field of my cell phone, and I wanted to say: "Hey, you know, if you want, I can take him off your hands." She'd laugh, and I'd laugh, then she'd admit she had no business taking care of the child she'd spent thirty or so weeks poisoning, and then he'd be home, and this nightmare would be done. That was the conversation I imagined, that was the conversation I rehearsed. Surely, she'd be ready to give him back any day now, but I guess my number sat unsent as well.

And so, I waited.

I shored up.

I researched.

I cried myself to sleep most nights, and I waited for her to need me.

CHAPTER 7

Co-Parenting 101

In retrospect, I'd say it took two weeks or so before I resolved to take matters into my own hands, so-to-speak. The ache of missing him and the worry sitting in the pit of my stomach came together in so much anxiety that I felt I could not breathe until I checked on him.

Against the advice of the courts, against the advice of my family and friends, I did what I shouldn't, and I reached out. To stay away was unthinkable. The court had given him back with wrongful impunity, and I'd been treated like a glorified nanny for those six months. Feeding him, clothing him, loving him, while they were poised to pull the rug out from me all along. I couldn't accept that. I couldn't accept that after waiting a lifetime, a half a year is all I got.

"Hi, Montaya," I surprised myself. Not a waver, not a tremor to give away the emotion I felt. I wanted to keep the pleading from my voice, but begging, at this point, I did not deem beneath me. I would have said anything, promised anything, just to hold him again. The court said he wasn't mine; I knew otherwise.

We made small talk, chatted about how much I missed him. With that conversation, I could feel something developing. A system, unstated, un-negotiated, but still there beneath the surface of our words. We each had something the other one wanted, the question was: what were each of us prepared to do to get it?

At the time, I wouldn't have hesitated to admit there was almost nothing for which they could ask that I would not grant. Looking back, I could not know, that for the next six years, I would indeed do anything and then some, in the name of that child.

But for now, Devon was not lost. I knew where he was, and with permission from his biological mother (I still couldn't bear to call her his mom or mommy). I was given permission to see him sometime.

In the beginning, it was simple. Finding in me a willing babysitter, Montaya found more and more reasons to let me pick him up for the night, the weekend, or most of the week if things at the motel or if house was without electricity.

I rejoiced in these opportunities, happy for any reason at all to have my son back home with me. I celebrated each and every moment with him, ever conscious of the fact it could be taken away any moment. Fear, as much as love, drove me in those early days. It was fear that found me digging into my pockets to pay for gas on a car I did not drive, or room fare for a hotel I would never step foot in.

Ultimately, it was fear that propelled us into a toxic symbiosis from which neither of us could safely or easily extricate ourselves. We both loved him, I never doubted that. But one day it would have to be made clear; only one of us could have him.

Like most co-parenting relationships -- for that's what we were, really -- we struggled to find common ground amongst our parenting styles, but we made it work. Milestones, birthdays, church, preschool, were all worked out together, and financed with my money.

Outwardly, I'm sure we made a strange trio, but whether I liked it or not, wanted it or not--we were family--at least until I could do something about it. So, as was my custom, I waited. I documented, I saved every receipt, every message, every scrap of evidence I thought might be useful someday, and I waited. I didn't know what I was waiting for, but something in my spirit told me to be still.

In the eyes of the court, I had no rights, no say, and no support. From the moment I picked up the phone to reach out to Montaya, I knew I was alone. Any moment, she and Wayne could decide they'd had enough of sharing, and shut their door against me and my love for Devon. I knew one day they would ask for more than I could give, and the baby between us would pay for my failure, but I was in too deep. I could no more walk away now than I could have six months prior, and I prayed for the Lord to guide my steps.

I could see pity in the eyes of my friends and some of my loved ones. I simply shook them off like so many drops of water and got on with what I had to do. It hurt me, I won't lie and say it didn't. I liked being thought well-of and being seen as a victim hurt my confidence a bit, but I pressed on. Yes, I knew that Montaya and Wayne were using me, but I was also using them to keep Devon safe. If they were my path to Devon, then I would gladly walk it to get to him, and never once did I feel shame in that.

I once heard it said: "We do what we have to do until we can do what we want to do." At that moment in time, I did what I had to do.

"Why do you do that?" my sister Patricia asked me on a night out. We were celebrating Devon's birthday, and as always, getting the family I had, and the family I'd made, together at one time, always led to issues.

"Why do I do what?" The pressure of putting the birthday together had been taxing enough. I would never be what you call "crafty," and the entire ordeal had no doubt made me snippier than

I'd intended, but yet another criticism from my big sister was the last thing I needed.

"You fawn and simper after Montaya like a slave," she spat, throwing a glance in Montaya's direction to make sure the target of her damning observation was present. "It's disgusting the way you let her treat you, Carla." And though I knew she thought she meant well, it did nothing to soothe the already frazzled exterior of my nerves.

"I don't act like a slave for anybody," I said to her, letting my tone act as a warning. Devon's birthday party was neither the time nor the place for such a discussion, and I refused to participate anyhow.

"You get her plate, make sure she has every little thing that she needs, but you should be enjoying Devon, your son's birthday not making sure Montaya is having a good time."

I shook my head in disbelief. This was exactly why I tried so hard to shield us from the judgment of others. I had it under control, but everyone, especially Pat, always thought they knew better when they knew nothing. "She's family, Devon's mother." I drew a breath for patience before continuing.

"No," Pat shook her head, not allowing me to even finish my thought, "no, she is not family. We did not sign up to see this woman run you into the ground. We didn't sign up to have every special occasion, holiday, or family visit, invaded by her presence. She is using you up, Carla, and you just let her."

"Miss Carla!" I could hear Montaya's voice rise above the din of the party as if to aid my sister in her argument. "Miss Carla, where Devon's presents go?!" She hollered, impatience creeping ever so slightly into her voice. Montaya was a mighty fine actress, and in front of my family, she was the picture of meekness and manners. It was always, "yes, Miss Pat," if she were speaking to my sister, or "yes, ma'am" if she was talking to my mom. But still, I heard it. I looked around the party room, confused about the question in general, never mind my irritation with my sister.

"It'd be nice to have your support, Pat," I said, still combing the room for Devon's missing presents. I stopped a second, letting a smile lift my cheeks as my eyes settled on my baby. He was such a sweet little boy and looked so happy there amongst the half-eaten cake and balloons.

"Well, I'm sorry," Pat said, looking as tired as I felt. "But, I'm never going to support anyone hurting you. I put Devon's presents in my car, by the way. Quick, go and tell Montaya before you get into trouble."

TEXT FROM MONTAYA

A: Are you STILL OK to get him, Mrs. Carla, I just woke back up just wanna b sure

C: Yes ma'am. I'm good to get him. Thank you for checking. Relax and Rest.

A: OK thank you once more ur a great co-parent love u much I'm serious thank u soo much

C: Thank you!

A: Yw now that part is the honest to god truth on my mom u are a great coparent amen thank u lord no matter wat ive said or done that's what the truth is.

CHAPTER 8

Almost Lost Him...
Again

Though we had fashioned an uneasy peace between us, there were few topics that would strain the fragility of our relationship like the topic of Devon's health. As a reasonably healthy person myself, I was often appalled at the more lackadaisical approach Montaya took with our son's care. It was during those times, when her basic parenting know-how was challenged, that my place as a "co" parent was most heavily emphasized.

Some months into our new arrangement, Devon contracted MRSA, and in my entire life, I have never felt more helpless. The amenability I tried so hard to maintain faltered under the stress of our son's declining health, and our relationship grew toxic, lapsing more and more into pettiness and power games.

"What you doin' here white girl?"

The twist of her lips let me know she thought herself clever. "White girl" had been my moniker since the beginning of our relationship. My light skin, "good hair," and polite mouth spat in the face of every convention governing her existence. Without the stamp of abuse, poverty, and struggle etched into the lines of my face, I lacked credibility. I could never be a mother to her child; I had no right to fish in her waters and not a day went by that she did not remind me.

I declined to answer her question directly. History taught me that Montaya was less interested in the obvious answer, and far more interested in a specific response. My only weapon was to give her neither and pray she'd busy herself with some other task. What I was "doin'" there was the same thing I've always done: being a mother to my son.

I watched my baby hooked up to the rubber tubes and flat sharp edges of machinery that beeped and pulsed his vitals onto a little screen. With his eyes closed, I wondered what peace, if any, could be found behind those soft, brown lids. Did he see me? Did he hear my voice calling him back into my arms, back to the home I worked so hard to create for him? I searched his face like a map, sought a steady course upon which to ground myself, and kept careful watch over the many storms Montaya tried to create within him.

She humphed her way into the room, reeking of sweat, and I heard the tell-tale rattle of a cold in the back of her hateful throat. "Are you sick?" I asked her carefully, knowing to question Queen Montaya was to invite a quarrel. I also knew a sick visitor could hurt my baby and snatch with greedy hands the progress he had quietly struggled to make.

"What?" She looked at me sharply, pausing her grand entrance, perhaps detecting the warning in my voice.

I squared my shoulders, prepared to fight if need be. "If you're sick, you can make him worse," I softened my tone in hopes that my concern for "our" son might temper the anger I saw flicker beneath her flesh.

"I am his mother," she thumped her chest on the "I" for emphasis as if to remind me the time I spent with my child was granted solely by her whims and generosity. What I did not hear in the echoes of her arrogant "I" was an acknowledgment of my claim to the child between us. It might have been her deficient womb that birthed him, but it was from my heart, my pocket, and the entirety of myself that he was loved and cared for.

Again I said nothing. To agree was to lie, and to correct was an invitation to an argument I could ill-afford in the wake of my son's health. I chose instead to instruct. "When you come into this room, you need to wash your hands. If you're sick, you need to stay away, or at the least wear a mask so your germs don't jeopardize his progress. He," I pointed to his small, still form underneath the thin hospital blanket, "needs to get better."

Her eyes slid away from "her son" quickly as if he were something that could be addressed later, and I could see at once that this wasn't to be a conversation about *him;* as always, it was to be a conversation about *her.* "So I'm trying to hurt my boy, is that it?" She narrowed her eyes and settled her spine into the large, soft swell of her hips. A born fighter, her features seemed to relax at the mere suggestion of confrontation. "You think you love him more, white girl? Oh, you got money, so whatever you say go, and I'm just s'posed to sit here and listen to you tell me how to care for *my* child? I have raised ten children," she spat at me," how many you got?"

I didn't take the bait. This same point of discussion came up often, and its sting had significantly lessened. As usual, Montaya loved only to glorify herself, even in the face of all common sense, truth, or fact.

Fact: She had been pregnant over 25 times, her body rejecting those poor souls not strong enough to survive the toxic air surrounding her blighted planet.

Fact: All ten of her other issues had, at some point, been taken away from her to varying degrees of success by the system she worked so tirelessly to exploit.

"I have one," I spoke evenly, my eyes locked onto the filmy, sick yellows of hers.

"Bit--" She started, advancing toward me in the temperature neutral stillness of his room. I took a flinching step backward, but not in fear, merely to increase my proximity to my son and decrease her access to a flag she was too ignorant to surrender.

A metallic *click!* Swiveled our collective attention to the door as a nurse, cart in tow, swished her way into the room.

Neither mine, nor Montaya's posture had relaxed even a centimeter in the wake of her blue-clad interruption, and the nurse, all too familiar with our dynamic, immediately set about neutralizing the tension with talk of him.

"How's our boy today?" She chirped brightly, her eyes asking the question her tone did not. *Are you okay?* I gave a quick nod to let her know all was well and eyed the contents of his tray. I noticed immediately the regimented quality of his portions and felt the thin heat of disgust shift beneath my cheeks.

Since his admittance into the hospital, Montaya had rummaged through my son's room as one might a pantry in their home. Formula, blankets, bottles, pillows--anything at all she could get her hands on, became the property of Queen Montaya, Inc. Never mind the cost of these items was indeed paid by *someone*. She was entitled to them because she was entitled to anything. By virtue of her struggle, her exploited *black*ness, her exploited *female*ness, her abused and wasted life, she was entitled to everything. It was her way, I think, of settling a score that could never really be satisfied.

"Y'all gon' starve my baby," she brayed, interrupting my quiet inventory, and startling the nurse from her clipboard. She eyed the sparse contents of his tray like a jeweler eyes the flaws in a diamond, her mouth turned down in observable disdain.

As was custom, the nurse said nothing to Montaya directly, merely regarded her as a small child asking a silly question and turned her back. The pecking order had long been established, and the nurse knew to direct all useful information to me: his mother.

Despite a setback and a series of touch-and-go moments that left me genuinely fearful for his life, eventually, my baby pulled through. Weaker, and minus a testicle, little by little he climbed his way back to us. If I could say anything about Montaya -- and by this point, I could say a lot -- she had given birth to a fighter; a fact for which I was eternally grateful, as he would no doubt need that fierce spirit in order to survive her.

CARD FROM DEVON'S PRE-K TEACHERS

Dear Mrs. Carla,

We wanted you to know how much we appreciate your support. You are such a POSITIVE in Devon's life. Have a wonderful summer.

Love,

Mrs. Taylor and Mrs. Lambert

CHAPTER 9

Who Is In Control?

"You know what the white liver is?"

In the time since Devon's hospitalization, things had more or less gone back to "normal," or what represented "normalcy," as we had come to know it. She and the rest of her family's demands on my time and resources had become uncomfortable, to say the least, but I was reluctant to cut all ties just yet.

Montaya and I were sitting on the filthy cushions of a couch purchased with my money in a house I owned. Trash, dust, grime, the hallmarks of neglect, were apparent everywhere I looked. I had purchased the home for a simple reason: my baby needed some place to live when he wasn't with me.

No one: Not Montaya, nor her boyfriends, worked for a living. They'd built their family name upon the shaky ground of "the system," and in so doing lived a life of prideful, almost imperial poverty. On the far too frequent occasions my son was with her, I feared for him. I feared for his environment; under what squalid conditions would she attempt to "raise" him? I feared for his safety; who or what would have access to him? What sordid individuals would be allowed to quietly usurp the good I worked tirelessly to instill within him? And so, I bought my baby a house to keep him close to me.

"Are you listening to me girl?" Ever the performer, Montaya hated to have any less than your full attention at any time. In this way she was not unlike a greedy child grabbing hungrily at the teat of your focus, mouth smacking incessantly at a worn and depleted nipple. Detecting that I may not be interested (how dare I) she'd heaved the full weight of her body in my direction, a sign of intimacy and secretiveness I didn't much care for. Though I had no idea what "white liver" could or might be, I had the vague notion that it was something unpleasant.

I'd come over that day to bring food, small items of entertainment for my baby, and to quietly survey her living conditions. I hadn't planned on staying long but plans rarely mattered with Montaya and there was no such thing as a "casual exchange." Montaya greeted me with a wide, wet smile at the door, and I deduced it was to be one of *those* visits. On these occasions, gone was the aggressive and haughty demeanor to which I had long grown accustomed. This Montaya was sweet, almost saccharine in her eagerness to "chat." Gone the animosity that so often prowled the shadows of our conversation. This Montaya was my *friend*. This Montaya wanted something.

"No." I shook my head firmly, mouth pursed in discomfort disguised as interest. It seemed that she was determined to educate me no matter my answer, so I'd decided honesty was best. "No," I repeated with a barely concealed sigh, trying hard to keep the irritation I felt out of my voice. "What is that?"

Her eyes flashed to mine with a twinkle, lip curled in so predatory a fashion I felt my cheeks flush in warning.

"Oh I bet you know," she cackled at me knowingly, head thrown back. She ran an oily palm down the front of her dress suggestively, lingering on the wide expanse of her breasts. "The white liver is when you want *it*, but you can't never get enough. Why you think I got so many men?" She jerked her thumb toward a back room, the sound of a video game echoed dimly from somewhere and floated its way through the filmy air back up to us. "They ain't worth nothing though," she slapped her knee and barked out a short ugly laugh. "Hell, I need me bout four or five of em' to make one decent one," she wiggled her gray coated tongue at me luridly as she continued to giggle.

Montaya, Devon's father (her ex-boyfriend), Wayne, and another boyfriend who lived in the house part-time all shared the space with a revolving door of related and non-related people at any given time. These men were in addition to her husband she was still legally married to (currently in prison). The filth my son was no doubt privy to clenched my stomach. Dysfunction and discord were everywhere I settled my eyes, and I could not -- would not -- simply walk away. I wondered what sort of man (ha!), what sort of men would take a woman, who hadn't been seen fit to raise her own children, who used a slop jar so she didn't have to get out of her own bed to take care of her bodily needs, and see in her a lover. In addition to the disgust I felt at her lifestyle, there was a real fear for Devon's safety as well. Abuse and perversion seemed to be a disease that infected nearly every member of her family, and I worried its crimson stain would spread to him if I let him tarry for too long.

Slipping away from my thoughts, I returned to Montaya, cocked my head, but said nothing. I was surprised, but not shocked; never that. Often, whenever she felt bored or just personally dissatisfied, I suspect, Montaya sought to subordinate me through shock. I, the sheltered "white girl," provided so much sport in this regard that I learned simply never to *be* shocked. Each conversation, it seemed to me, was a play for power in some way; a way to gain or regain footing on the rocky terrain of our relationship. "Shock," I learned early on, could easily morph into sympathy, which could then be exploited and monetized.

I was "shocked" when she told me horrible accounts of the abuse she'd suffered as a child. Each lurid detail hammered me with guilt as I could, in return, only offer tales of a childhood spent in the Midwest, safe amongst flat green lawns and two loving parents. Because I could not match her suffering, I let it charm me instead. Every story found me digging into the worn pockets of my wallet or the well of my purse. Because I could not change what had been done to her, I bought clothes, I bought food, I bought everything. I also gave her what money couldn't buy: the attention she craved with an insatiable thirst.

"Interesting." I adjusted my posture, the only sign I'd allow that what she said had any effect on me, but kept my face neutral. "What about it, Montaya?"

"Well," her tone grew conspiratorial like we were just two gals gabbing about our love-lives, "it might help if I had some toys to play with." Her eyelid slid closed in a wink and I felt my stomach lurch in disgust.

"I'm not sure that's something you need to discuss with me," I said with a snort that felt less than friendly. "That's your business, girl."

She'd settled back into the greasy cushions of the couch with all the composure of a queen. She'd made her request clear and waited patiently for it to become clear to me as well. "So you don't never get lonely up in that big ol' house with no man?" She asked the question on the edges of a smile and I knew she was teasing, actively trying to make me uncomfortable.

Before I could throw on the mask I'd crafted especially for these occasions, I felt myself blush. Her comment, though silly, only worked to reinforce the dynamic she'd created between us. I was a bland, sexless, barren, *white woman*, valuable only for my money. I could see *her* pity *me* and it infuriated me. "I'm too busy with *my* baby to be worried about some mess like that," I answered brusquely, tired already of her games.

I saw my comment hit home. Practiced in the art of aggressive negotiations, it wouldn't do for her to display her anger to me, but I saw it. I saw it the narrowing of her eyes and the flare of her nostrils. I'd pissed her off.

"Oh, I see," she answered sagely as if anticipating this very response. "You too good."

"No--"

"No," she cut me off, her anger building momentum, lending her words a speed and fluidity not often present in our interactions. "Maybe," she continued, "if I spent more time with my son, then I wouldn't be worried about some mess like that." She mimicked nastily, her face screwed up in a baleful reflection of my own. "You always comin' up in here thinking you better than somebody." Her arms had crossed, a sturdy "X" made of flesh and bone in front of her chest which now heaved up and down in angry bursts. No longer were we "pals," but two women on opposite sides of a divide that went deeper than the child at the center of our relationship. I had *offended* her.

She stood up, the couch groaning under her weight and effort. "I think you need to get going," she said dismissively, not bothering to look me in the eye. Our business was done. "We got family things to do," and nodded her head toward my front door.

I could leave, but I also knew what would happen if I did. It might be days before she let me see my baby again. My love for him superseded any humiliation or manipulation she could possibly devise, so I did what I always did. I stayed. I waited for her to tell me what I could do to make up for the fact that I would always have more power, but for the time being, she had him.

"I'm sorry," I said tiredly. "I didn't mean anything by it, Montaya, you just surprised me that's all." I tried hard to soften my voice, return once more to the frivolity of a moment ago. Rather than let the moment hang between us, I busied myself with clean up, any excuse to get up and not meet her gaze. I stacked cups, shuffled napkins, and waited for it to pass.

"It's alright, white girl," she laughed at my obvious naïveté, dismissed me with a wave of her hand and a flash-fried grin. "So you gon' get me some?"

I stared, startled for a moment, not entirely sure what "some" was. "Some what?" I'd stopped cleaning and stood motionless in the living room, a crumpled napkin still in my hand.

"Tsk," she sucked her teeth and rolled her eyes at me. "Some toys," she said plainly as if it were the most natural request in the world. I could almost feel her exasperation which only deepened my incredulity.

I thought about it. I thought about walking into one of those stores I'd seen around town or having an item like that delivered directly to my home and it shamed me, as I'm sure it was meant to. I could say no. The option was always mine, but not really, right? To say *no* to Montaya in her times of want and need was a *yes* to something far worse. Given the particular context of our conversation, I couldn't imagine what worse thing might be lurking in her sub-text.

"Okay," I said evenly, "what would you like?"

The smile she gave me suggested gratitude, but I saw it for what it was: Victory.

MONTAYA: FACEBOOK POST

I'm still out here located in bank [of] America parking lot haven't eaten in a couple days done [suffered] another light stroke got heat rash from sitting at Auto zone all day waiting for [Wayne] to make room fare but I spent my hold 1200 making sure we all have a place to live and paying decks buying cigarettes, beer, dope and feeding everyone, but I can't even enjoy a sandwich by myself got put out of the Cadillac earlier Wayne called me all out my name but yet I'm the one who holds it down and make sure they straight...life a Bitch then we die I'm all tired of this bull shit I'm sicking tired of beening sick and tierd.

CHAPTER 10

Money & Manipulation

$6,625.00

I stared down at the numbers in disbelief. The dates read from March 1 through April 1- just a month, but each itemized entry felt like the cold, precise cut of a razor.

$1500 PayPal transfer court 3/1

$2800 car 3/4

$100 cash 3/5

$280 cash court 3/11

$200 Walmart card 3/11

$100 cash 3/12

$40 cash Wayne 3/13

....and on and on.

In loving and caring for my son, there were so many things for which I had prepared myself: I prepared myself to love a child that would never look like me, wouldn't have my father's charming smile, or my mother's sweet nature. I prepared to look in the mirror and never see the stamp of motherhood on my body for a child that filled so much of my heart. What I could not, did not prepare for, was the assault on my time, money, and generosity by my son's birth family.

Sitting at my kitchen table, in my beautiful house, I felt proud. Proud of the life I'd created for myself, and my accomplishments. Through prayer, the support of my family, and hard work, I'd created a home in which to raise my child, and I seethed at their gall. Each dollar sign branded my spirit, filled me with a coldness I found alarming.

My success enraged them. In their eyes, all that I had, I shouldn't, and they sought at every turn to punish me for achieving what they could not. How dare I overcome the obstacles they'd so willingly allowed to stall them. My education, money, and upbringing made an enemy of me, and their attacks upon my livelihood were relentless.

The items on my bank account went further than mere abuse; they seemed to speak to something much darker, a dangerous entitlement that sought to monetize my love of *their* child. Forty dollars here, twelve hundred there, all paid for the pleasure of being with *my* son. Oh, I could have him, but I would have to pay. It was the worst kind of cruelty--to exploit the resources I used to care for a child they couldn't.

The few times they'd been inside my home I watched their jealous eyes slide over every stick and thread of my belongings. "You got it going on Miss Carla!" Montaya exclaimed, struggling to turn a sneer into a smile. "Who she think she is?" Their hands seemed to say as they caressed my counter tops, imagining themselves in my place. I understood from their straight backs and polite rejection of refreshment, that they hated me.

I pushed the handful of statements and their hateful numbers away and got up to prepare my lemon water. Never much of a drinker, I didn't keep so much as a bottle of wine in the house, but, the refreshing tang of the citrus infused water, relaxed me as much as any glass of red or white could have. I could hear my baby upstairs, safe in the room I'd so lovingly decorated and felt a peace come over me. Devon spent at least 80% of his time with me now, and though the six grand (for that month) sickened me, I would've paid more. Leaning against my counter, I ran a tired hand through my hair and really had to stop and laugh at the absurdity of his biological parents.

"You can get me something to eat?" his father, Wayne would often ask when I stopped by the house. Even the way he asked, a question of my ability to feed him versus a request to be fed, spoke volumes about the people responsible for my son's genetic identity. In their world, there was an unchallenged expectation of assistance. If you had it and they didn't, why then would you not help them? So, it was never really a question of: *could* you do it? Of course you would. The only real question was: *would* you do it, and if so, how soon?

An immeasurable sadness would come over me during these exchanges. How could a person live like this? I often wondered. What chance, if any, would my baby have had, if left solely in their care? I thought of him and so many other children who were born without a chance simply due to the poor choices of their birth parents and the circumstances that led to those choices. I thought about all the brown faces I'd seen recently in the news and wondered how many of them were going home to mothers like Montaya and fathers like Wayne. I worried about my own brown son, looking across the middle console of my car at what would surely be his future if something wasn't done to save him.

Another part of me felt contempt. Why was it my responsibility to make sure this grown man ate, or make sure his cell phone bill was paid, or that he had gas in his tank? I looked at the life they lived, due in large part to the money I was willing to throw at their bottomless greed, and marveled at a group of people so deeply embedded in my pocket still having the audacity to challenge my role in Devon's life. It was at these moments I tried hard to remember the person my parents raised me to be: kind, with a servant's heart.

"I can do that," I answered simply. And that really was the long and short of it. I could do it, so I would. "What do you want?"

"Couple cheeseburgers," he'd already started making his way to my car. Wayne had ceased to intimidate me long ago and filled me now with irritation more than anything. His intense hatred of both women and "the man" made him seem more weak than menacing, and while he may not mind spending my money, any attempt to claim it as mine would surely upset him. Besides, I was a woman. It was my job to take care of him.

I spoke very little on the way to the drive-thru. Unsure of his position when around me, Wayne sought to fill the space with talk. Talk of his plans, which often never amounted to much, complaints about Montaya and how crazy she was, pride in how big Devon was getting; just talk, really.

"I want two cheeseburgers and a milkshake," he interjected suddenly, interrupting his own monologue. "You asked for two cheeseburgers Wayne," I reminded him, not unlike the way I chided Devon when he asked for more than what was offered.

"What you mean?" He turned to me, hands up with palms out in inquiry.

"I mean," I answered slowly, "that you only asked me for two cheeseburgers, and that's all I'm prepared to buy." I didn't take my eyes off the road in front of me, needing to make my intention and resolve clear: I would not be taken advantage of. Though small in theory, the milkshake came to represent, in that moment, the wanton undermining of my power in regards to our relationship. I was Devon's mother, not an ATM on which to punch in a demand and expect immediate payment.

"Tsk," he sucked his teeth and withdrew from me, pushing himself as tightly into the corner of the passenger seat as possible. I could hear the seat belt pull and lock against the sudden movement as I rolled up to the drive-thru and waited.

"So you want the burgers?" I asked mildly, trying to shift the tone of our interaction in a more positive direction. I wasn't mad; I just wasn't buying any milkshakes.

"Man, forget it," he said tightly, not looking at me. I was taken aback at just how angry he had become and stopped my car more out of disbelief than anything else. That this man -- how this grown man with children, and for all intents and purposes, a wife, could become so angry at me for not buying him a milkshake really baffled me. In his mind, I could see that he felt he *deserved* the milkshake by virtue of his desire for it and that was enough reason to expect it. But this is how it was. A "no," no matter how reasonable, could change so much so quickly. I had to look no further than his father to see the origin of this behavior in my son.

"I'll get you the burgers if you--"

"I said forget it, I don't need nothing," he cut me off and turned his head to the window, indicating there was nothing more to say. And really? What more was there?

He didn't speak to me again for another two weeks.

VOICE MESSAGE
FROM MONTAYA

...DSS came and got my baby from this motherfucking school. But it's all good. If I – goddamn -- I lose my motherfuckin' boy you goddamn better look for it. I'm coming to kill you, and then I'm gonna kill my goddamn self. And then I'm gonna kill a couple other people; you better believe that. Now take that to the fuking bank. I'm not motherfucking playing."

CHAPTER 11

I'm OK

Though being a mother was and is the joy of my life, parenthood, no matter how it comes about, presents with more than a few difficulties. I was blessed, beyond measure, to have both a niece and nephew who grew up to have great success in life and love. And eventually it came time to celebrate with a wedding; specifically, my nephew.

My niece, Danielle, had gotten married earlier in the year, and I was pleased to be a part of her ceremony as the Maid of Honor. Less than a year later, my nephew, Andrew, was poised to add another member to our family. The only problem? He and his bride had decided on a chic ceremony in Washington D.C.: no kids allowed.

The question became: with whom could I entrust the care of my son, who at the age of six, already carried within him such anger and violence? The level of patience and care Devon needed for an entire weekend without me was far too large a favor to ask of just anyone. The one girlfriend I might have allowed to help me had her own plans for the weekend in question, and what I absolutely would not consider was the aid of Montaya and Wayne.

I knew to say no would cause harm, would break trust. I knew how my family would feel: that I put this child, who wasn't even mine, before them, a family I had been a part of all my life, and in a sense it was true. I would be willing to hurt them, break plans, do whatever I had to do because he is my son. The decision to miss my nephew's wedding hurt me deeply, and every happy photo on social media anchored heavy hooks of guilt within me. But that's where I was in my journey: isolated and alone.

How could I make my nephew, my sister, anyone, really, understand the holistic misery of my struggles as a single mother of a foster child? Every abuse, exploitation, and indignity I encountered at the hands of Montaya, Wayne, and an unrepentant system, left me more and more secluded.

I had turned into a woman with an apology always at the ready.

I'm sorry, I can't make it.

I'm sorry, I can't do that.

I'm sorry, we won't be there.

My primary role as Devon's mother had always been that of protector. I tried to protect him from the wicked influence of his birth parents, protected him from the cruel impressions of the world, and when it was necessary, I protected him from himself. But there wasn't anyone protecting me.

There was no partner for me to cry on the shoulder of at night after a long day of fighting the world. There wasn't anyone to share the weight when it became too heavy, and no one to stay behind when something important came up: no matter who or how much it hurt.

As a way to smooth things over, I'd agreed to meet my family in Indiana, where my mother and father still lived. My sister, my niece and her new husband, my nephew and his new wife, and along with me, my baby.

Montaya had reluctantly given me permission to take him across the country. North Carolina to Indiana was no small excursion, and I was grateful for the weekend she'd given me.

"Take care of my baby," she'd said without even the ghost of a smile as I ushered him into the backseat. I assured her that I would, I didn't add that I *always* did.

Not long into our trip, her tune changed substantially.

Bring my baby back!

Bitch, I didn't say you could take him!

The text messages she sent nearly non-stop hour after hour glowed hotly in my inbox, and finally, I put my phone on silent to quiet the metallic buzzing of my phone.

Though I enjoyed the company of my family, and I loved for Devon to get to know me and himself through them, Montaya's presence hovered around us like a tortured poltergeist. Every single hour was punctuated by the shrill alert of my phone letting me know that I'd missed another frantic text or hysterical phone call.

Why don't you just ignore her? A constant refrain from the members of my family. I could see it beginning to wear on them. They saw the tired smile and darkened hollows beneath my eyes, and while I knew they wanted to help--they couldn't. It was always something, and beneath their concern, I saw something else: they were annoyed. They had no idea what I was going through. I couldn't just ignore her any more than I couldn't make her *not* Devon's mother and her endless dramatics were mine to bear alone, no matter how *annoyed* they were.

Hoping to talk some sense into her, at the very least, talk her into leaving us alone to enjoy our trip, I finally relented and called her.

"Put my baby on the phone!" She screamed, it seemed, from the very streets of North Carolina. "I didn't say you could take him anywhere." To a novice, the despair in her voice might have seemed genuine, a mother fearful for her child, desperate to get him back. But I knew better. This was about control, and with me so far away and Devon out of her reach, she had none. This call was a cry for attention, nothing more

"Montaya," I reassured her in as calm a voice as I could manage, "you did say I could take him. We talked about this." I found sometimes the best way to deal with her nonsense was to make short statements of fact rather than emotional declarations.

"Well I changed my mind," she continued, entirely unfazed by my version of our conversation leading up to this vacation. "I already called the police," she finished dramatically, silent in an effort to gauge my response. I could almost hear her thinking, *Well, what do you think of that?*

"Why would you call the police?" I knew the tone of my voice was sharp, but the idea of being confronted here, by the police, in the home of my elderly parents, was nearly too much to bear. "Why would you do that?" I repeated.

"I called the police because you won't picking up the phone. You kidnapped my baby and you need to bring him home!" She screamed this last statement into the phone loud enough to make it vibrate against my ear.

This statement didn't feel true, but then again, I couldn't ever tell with her. Lying came as easily as breathing, and a lie was nothing for her to tell if it served even a tenth of her interests.

As I listened to her rant and rave, cuss words flowing like water through my phone as she blessed me out, I really had to stop and wonder what this tantrum was actually about.

On the one hand, she was almost certainly lying. On the other, I couldn't risk a charge like that in my quest for eventual custody of Devon. Considering the punishingly strict family court laws in North Carolina as they pertained to foster families and adoption, particularly when my foster parenting rights had been terminated, I could ill-afford to draw the ire of the court on a matter as simple as an approved family vacation.

"Put my son on the phone." Her voice was so hot and tight, the anger nearly coiled around her words. I had a fairly strict, but in my opinion, straightforward approach to Devon keeping in touch with his birth parents: they could have as much access to him as they wanted when he was with me, but I refused to let him get sucked into any of their nonsense. And while her request to speak to Devon did seem incredibly unwise, I thought it might help quell some of the anger I heard in her voice. Sitting on the couch in my mother's living room, I reluctantly gave Devon my phone and hoped whatever drama Montaya was trying to manufacture would now be easily satisfied.

What the fuck is you doing?

I could hear her hateful voice spray like acid through the phone and into my child's ear. I cringed in embarrassment; my mother was seated next to us, and while I was used to such vile language from Montaya, and though I tried in vain to protect him, so was Devon, my sweet mother, on the other hand, was not, and I was furious. She had no place here.

When Devon grabbed my phone, he must have engaged the speaker and we all became a captive audience for the Montaya Show.

I don't give a fuck what she say. When I say get on the phone, get yo ass on the phone!

I could see my baby's face crumple. He'd been excited to talk to his MawMaw, excited to tell her about his trip, but as usual, she'd figured out a way to take it away from him. Instead of being happy that Devon was in the world, seeing new places and new things with people that loved him, she focused her energies on shaming him for it. If it didn't benefit her, then it would benefit no one.

"You listen to me," she said, continuing her assault on my baby's good time. "You ain't never gon' be better than us, you hear me? You have our blood running through your veins, and it don't matter where you go, or what you do, you always gon' be one of us." Devon stared straight ahead, saying nothing. A call like this could throw off his emotional balance and leave my son angry or sad for hours.

In three long strides, I was across the room and snatched my phone back from him. I wasn't sure what more she would say, but the idea that my mother could hear her speak to my son that way was more than I was willing to deal with, especially in light of her threat to have me arrested.

I thought about all the things I did for this woman and her family, and I couldn't help the anger in my heart. This wasn't how it was supposed to be. In a perfect world, there would be no Montaya. I could take my son on a family trip and watch him laugh with his cousins, get loved on by his aunt, and there'd be no threat to our peace, no thief to come steal our joy.

But the world was not perfect.

"You don't talk like that on my phone,"

My voice was on fire, ready to raze whatever discord she felt inclined to sow. How dare she call here and upset my son, upset my family?

"What you talkin' bout? Put Devon back on the phone," she said dismissively, seemingly unaware that she no longer had the upper hand; instead of entertaining herself with a cub, she now had the attention of a lioness.

"No," I stated simply. "He's not getting back on the phone. Do you know we can hear you? Hear the way you're talking to him? My mother is in this room right now, and she doesn't deserve to be subjected to your language. You need to get a hold of yourself, Montaya. You're being ridiculous."

"Okay, bitch I see," she attempted to reassert herself.

"You wanna play games. We'll see who's ridiculous when the PoPo come and pick yo ass up for kidnappin.'"

I hung up the phone.

They never came.

Imagine that.

The rest of our trip commenced without further incident, but the damage had been done. And really, that was the whole point, right? My father was a quiet man and tried hard to let us manage our affairs as adults without much interference, but even I could tell his fear and worry for me was nearly enough to break through his trademark stoicism. Every tantrum, every act of violence that Devon might display as a sign of distress, did not go unnoticed by my watchful father.

"What's going on," he asked me plainly, knowing that I wasn't telling him everything.

"Everything is alright," I smiled, trying to turn on the charm that worked when I was younger but failed in every way to engage him now.

"I'm worried about you, daughter," he looked me deep in my eyes, toothpick bouncing around his mouth, a replacement for the smoking habit he'd quit decades before. My father, still so handsome, even in his seventies, wavy hair, long past gray, waited patiently for me, his youngest, his baby girl, to tell him the truth.

"I'm okay," I replied, hugging him briefly, neither one of us quite able to believe it.

TEXT MESSAGE FROM MONTAYA

I'm giving my sister your address and she's coming to fuck you up.

CHAPTER 12

Breaking The Cycle

"How are you, Carla?" The question was simple. As always, the answer was not. Being a mother had brought me unrestrained joy, but with it came an anxiety I had not expected. The stress of dealing with Devon's birth parents, their financial and emotional manipulation, and the day to day struggle of being a single parent to a challenging child had left me emotionally bereft enough to seek the services of a counselor.

I wasn't one to wallow in my problems and followed the "I have it under control" principle of adulthood. If there were problems, I used my time, resources, and talents to solve those problems. But, there are only so many restless nights one can or should endure before admitting that the usual cure isn't fixing anything.

I needed objectivity. I didn't trust the opinions, advice, or observations of my friends and family. They had no idea what I was going through and it was far too risky to open myself up to their scrutiny. I felt it important to protect both myself and Devon from negative criticism, and to a certain degree, from meddling. I kept a lot of my struggle to myself because I knew I wouldn't be understood. My sister, Patricia, moved to Charlotte not long after I did, and while her presence was immeasurably helpful, it was in no way without judgment. Ever the big sister, I felt every conversation about Devon, the situation with his parents, and my choices in general, to be laden with the heavy subtext *of this is what you should do.* The expectation for me to follow her advice lockstep made it painfully difficult for us to communicate, and after many frustrating attempts, I stopped trying. I needed someone to look at my choices without value or emotion, and above all, I needed someone to listen to me. I needed to say the fears that plagued me both awake and sleeping, out loud.

I was afraid I might lose him.

I was afraid I might not get him back.

I was afraid I wasn't the mother he needed.

I was afraid I wasn't the mother he wanted.

I was afraid.

But there amongst the fear, hot and silent, peeking like a rabbit through the brush, was anger. I was angry at Montaya. I was angry at "the system" that made it absurdly difficult for me to be a mother to my child. I was angry at every person that commented on my "bravery" for taking on "a child like Devon."

So that's how I was today: angry and afraid.

"Have you thought about writing a letter?" The suggestion came after a particularly lengthy silence so I wasn't altogether prepared for it. As usual, the suggestion was delivered in an utterly neutral fashion, in total contrast to her bright and energetic office. I liked my therapist. She was young, still optimistic and wonderfully objective. She didn't recoil in horror at the things I shared with her, only responded with cool, academic interest. Even now, on the heels of such a bizarre suggestion, she seemed keen, but not expectant. She clutched a brightly patterned throw pillow against her brightly patterned shirt and said nothing, her Tom's-clad foot tapping patiently on a blue ottoman.

"A letter to whom?" I asked with some confusion and thinly veiled skepticism. I twisted uncomfortably in my seat, straightening my posture under her watchful gaze. What did I look like writing a letter? I imagined how I must seem to her. Fresh from one meeting and on my way to another, the suit I donned was tailored, but feminine and tasteful. I wore silver heels to echo the soft grays and pinks of my floral jacket and tried hard to exude professional detachment.

"To these concerns," she answered simply, sliding a lock of straight brown hair behind her ear. Maybe the act of putting down on paper the things that are troubling you might help you see them differently. If that's too abstract, then you can address the letter to whomever you'd like: Montaya, DSS, it doesn't matter. You never even have to mail it-it's just a matter of externalizing it, getting it out."

"I don't have to mail it?" Silly as it seemed, the idea did have some appeal, and who knew? It might make me feel better to see it all written down.

"Nope. Write it, seal it, and forget about it. The concerns won't disappear, obviously, but sometimes just putting things in a different place opens up all sorts of doors. Couldn't hurt, right? Now, how are your mom and dad?"

I answered, talked a bit about work, and our session was over. Another task checked off my list for the day. I thanked her and headed to my meeting, turning the idea over and over in my mind. A letter. I could do that. Obviously, I wouldn't mail it, but to whom should I address it? I drove through the wide clean streets of my city. I loved Charlotte. It was so pretty. All around me were bright green lawns and abandoned toys. I could see an echo of its genteel history in the rolling hills that danced around run-down strip malls and thriving businesses. It was the perfect place to raise my son, and I smiled at the thought of him, the letter forgotten for just a moment.

I breezed into the house after the conclusion of my meeting more than a little distracted. Determined to not let the direction of my thoughts lead me too far away from Devon, I made an effort to "reset," so he could have me unencumbered. Setting my things down, I scanned the living room for signs of him amongst the scattered toys, games, and books. "Devon!" I called out, making my way towards the kitchen. "Mommy's home."

"We're in here!" Devon's nanny called, just as I rounded the corner. I could only see about half of her, buried as she was deep in my refrigerator. "I was just getting ready to fix Devon a snack," she said, righting herself, greeting me with a smile, the corners of which seemed strained under the warm kitchen lights.

"What's up, where's Devon?" I'd expected to see him in the kitchen and was a bit surprised that he hadn't yet knocked me over in greeting.

"He's in his room playing on electronics," she waved a hand in the direction of the stairs and continued with Devon's snack: grapes and Doritos, two of his favorites. I left her to it and steered myself towards the stairs, sifting through mail absently as I walked. Something felt off.

I pushed gently on his door, calling his name softly as I entered. "Hey baby," I said, scooting next to him on his rumpled comforter. He was laying down on his belly, sock-clad feet in the air, eyes glued to the screen. Like any kid, screen-time was a constant struggle, and I tried to check my irritation that he'd already managed to get locked-in so soon after school. "Come give me a hug," I prodded gently, kissing him on his soft brown cheek.

"Leave me alone," he answered quietly, nudging me a bit, eyes never leaving his screen.

"What's the matter, baby?" I straightened up in confusion, not sure what I'd walked into. Things had certainly felt strained when I got home, but I hadn't gotten any frantic phone calls from his school, so no trouble there. My mind flicked to a million possible scenarios. Had Montaya or Wayne shown up here, shown up at his school? No, Janet would have let me know if anything like that had happened. She had strict instructions when it came to Devon's biological parents.

"Nothin'," he shrugged, settling the matter.

"Okay baby, but you can tell me anything," I slid slowly back down to the bed, wanting him to feel close to me, wanting him to know I was right here no matter where his thoughts had taken him. "Janet has a snack for you when you're ready okay?" I said brightly, in an effort to open him up. The digital beeps and ruckus from his screen were the only response he would offer and so I got up, feeling the distance between us as I crossed his room to leave.

"What's wrong with Devon? I decided against subtly and got straight to the point as I entered my kitchen. Devon's snack sat prettily on a plate at the table and I saw the makings of dinner already on the counter. I was blessed to have Janet and thanked God for her every day. She dutifully bore the challenges of our situation with such patience and love. I knew whatever plagued Devon was no fault of hers and thus waited for her answer with a respect borne of respect.

"Well," she began carefully, "I think Devon is just missing his birth family today." Her left shoulder shot up in a non-committal gesture, clearly uneasy as she set about getting dinner started. "I asked him if he missed his mommy today," she continued, "and he asked if I meant 'the good mommy or the bad mommy.' I asked which was which, and he told me that you," she pointed a spoon laden hand in my direction, "were the good mommy, and that Montaya was the bad mommy."

Internally I was relieved but saddened. This conflict wasn't new, but it pained me that he felt so obligated to draw such rigid lines in the sand when it came to his love for Montaya and me. Though it seemed clear that he was much better off in my care for a number of reasons, never did I ever want him to feel as if he couldn't love us both. "Did he say anything else?" I nodded, processing the information.

"No, not really," Janet sighed, wishing she could be of more help. "We worked on homework and he asked for his electronics. He seemed so sad I went ahead and said yes," she scrunched her face in apology, knowing my rules about screen time.

"That's alright," I smiled, letting her know I wasn't upset. "It won't hurt him." I got up from the table and let myself quietly into my office. Dinner would be ready soon and I just wanted a moment to think before the struggle of dinner, bath, and bedtime got sufficiently underway. I sagged into the cool upholstery of my desk chair and let the day run through me for a moment. I had a business dinner in the next two days for which I truly needed to prepare, but my mind kept returning to the letter my therapist suggested I write. It had initially seemed silly, but I wondered if now wouldn't be the best time to try; now when I had so many things to say and no one to say them to.

Opening the slim drawer of my desk, I pulled out a blank sheet of paper and a pen. My hands performed the movements automatically, my mind not yet sure of the task. I filtered through a literal barrage of thoughts and images, my fingers tapping a cheap BIC pen against a calendar spread before me. I thought about my baby's sad eyes upstairs in his room, and his struggle to love both his mothers without guilt. I thought of the receipts that proved every day I was being taken advantage of, and the daily threats I received when some new demand wasn't being met in a "satisfactory" amount of time. I let these thoughts and others settle over me, coating my skin like a thin layer of oil, picked up my pen, and begin to write.

"Dear," I stopped there, hovering over the word. Its implied intimacy and friendliness looked strange there against the stark white of my blank, naked page. I blinked away the tear I could feel inching its way from my eye and slashed a harsh line through the inappropriate salutation. Taking a moment to collect myself, I knew exactly what I wanted to say, and to whom I needed to say it.

Montaya,

Once pen was to paper and the initial "i" dotted, the words came smoothly, as if directed from a well within my spirit. I didn't know if she would ever see it, but the words were for her; they could no longer stay with me.

Montaya,

I just want a genuine drama-free relationship with you. Free of threats. Free of expectations that I cannot meet. From day one I told you that I would 100% take care of Devon. I am more than willing to take care of his education, experiences, and safety. Nothing is going to change that.

I told you that I would take care of the basics for you: food, clothing, and shelter; I have done that, and will continue to do that. What I will not do, is anything extra. You make certain choices and then get angry because you don't have money for what you need, let alone what you want. Too much of the focus is on material things and money. The next material thing isn't going to bring happiness to you, or to me, but especially not to Devon. Again, the money I give you is for food for Devon, not for anything else. If you don't want the money then throw it away. I don't need to hear about it.

I also don't need mean texts or voicemails. I don't need anyone coming to my house and causing a scene. My neighbors told me that you came banging on the door. You know that's not something you should do. No further comment needed on that. It cannot happen again. All of this drama keeps Devon scared and anxious and we both know that's not good. Any and everyone who is yelling, fussing, complaining, fighting, etc., has some ownership in making our baby anxious and it has to stop.

Devon shouldn't think it's ok to say he "hates", or to call people bad names, or to hit. The aggression comes from what he sees. And that has to change. I thought we agreed but every day now there's just more of it...more complaining about what's wrong and less being thankful for what's right. More cussin' and fussin'. Less being humble and grateful. More yelling and telling, less praying and fasting. More focus on who didn't do or did do. More about how bad something or someone is and less about the glory of God. I have to wake up daily with hope. I have to wake up being grateful. I cannot let anyone steal my joy. You used to do the same. I miss that gospel loving, Christian woman who wants to do better and who wants better for her son. Who prays before speaking, who is grateful for what has gotten better. And who is humble. Find her, please.

At the end of the day, I am constantly reminded I have no rights and no say so when it comes to Devon. Ok. So be it. I'm not going to be on a rollercoaster. I'm not going to fuss and fight, I only ever want what's best for him. That should be your aim as well. For Devon, I would give my life. I love him with all my heart. For me to provide for him and for you I must work. To work I need to be stable. To stay on my routine. Emergencies should not happen nearly as often as they do, and when they do, the routine is disrupted. For a real emergency, I will adjust my schedule. But not for daily drama.

Lastly, everything is not about you. Today is not about you. And if you choose to take Devon away from me, then we all have to live with that decision. I'm not begging, I'm not game playing, none of that. His life and well-being are too important to be used as a constant bargaining chip. He loves us both so much, we need to honor that. -Me

I looked down at the letter and waited to feel better.

CHAPTER 13

Trauma

W e'd had a rough day.

Now, with the evening's events behind us, right at the edge of bedtime, came a moment of tough reflection. Like any kid, my baby had his good and bad days. Today was bad.

Amongst the day's many challenges, we'd had a home visit from a new therapist, and with change always came confrontation. Sensitive for his age, any disruption to his normal schedule could shake and splinter an already fragile foundation.

I warned her, the well-meaning therapist, that her visit was likely to be met with open hostility and a less than cooperative attitude on his part. "That's okay," she said brightly, shrugging friendly shoulders. Her casual response was meant, surely, to assuage my fears, but was ultimately unsuccessful--I had been here often.

"I need to see the real Devon, she continued smiling in a way that suggested she was used to "unpleasantness." I was tired already, knowing what a handful the "real" Devon could be if he felt anxious or upset.

It didn't take long for my concerns to become realized as I watched my son, who could be so sweet and loving despite all he'd been through, throw his toys across the room and scream "Bitch, I don't like you!" at the top of his lungs as the therapist jotted down notes--her smile never wavering.

"Can I have my iPad mommy?" He later asked after the therapist had left for the evening.

"No you cannot play on your iPad," I'd said gently to his request. His behavior with the therapist had not only been predictably terrible but overly so. Things had not gone much better despite the therapist's many efforts to charm him and frankly, he'd really shown out. And so, like any mother, I'd been forced to make a choice based on this.

Perhaps where any other child might've shrugged off this punishment, chalked it up to the ebb and flow of a healthy parent/child relationship-my baby could not do that. Rejection of any kind could darken the sunniest of skies and snatch my sweet child away from me within minutes.

"I'm bad," he'd said to me as we made our way toward bedtime and lights out.

"Why would you say that, baby?" I asked him, closing our book of affirmations. The story of a self-doubting dolphin had become part of our nightly bedtime ritual, but the feel-good words of Jellyfish and Hermit Crab were no match for the self-doubt inside my baby's heart that evening.

"Because I'm not good," he answered quietly. "I feel like I'm going to--," he stopped to point down at the floor and I knew he meant hell. He'd made similar claims before, but it never ceased to surprise or hurt me to know my little boy so often carried that heavy a load on his heart. While other children worried about getting sent to their room, or not getting dessert, my baby worried about eternal damnation and the state of his soul. "I wanna go live with MawMaw," he continued, picking at a thread on his Panther's bedspread. Silver, black, and blue decorated every surface of his room--the colors of his beloved Panthers. His hero, Cam Newton, watched over him from a life-sized poster near his bed, but even here, safe in the space I'd made for him, he wasn't quite free of the evil Montaya tried so hard to put in him.

"Hey, what does the Angelfish say? "I nudged him, referencing our abandoned book trying to get us back on track. He didn't answer, just stared sullenly at the Panther blue walls of his room. "The Angelfish says…." I prompted, hoping that if he heard himself echo the self-love of the fictional fish, it would start to feel true.

"I wanna go live with MawMaw," he repeated, cutting me off, choosing not to say what we both needed to hear. 'I love myself,' was the line, but it seemed Angelfish was alone in that sentiment tonight.

"Well, why do you want to go live with MawMaw," I asked, interested in the path he seemed determined to walk. "What kind of things would you do there?"

"If I lived with MawMaw, then I could do bad stuff." He looked at me finally, a challenge rippling the flesh of his soft, round face. Though I could never respect Montaya as a person, or as a mother, I made myself acknowledge her place in his life and kept my lips closed against her when in his presence. He would not get the fight he was angling for from me.

"I see," I probed carefully, aware that my response could quell or accelerate the trouble I saw ahead. "What sorts of bad things?"

"I could smoke dope and be gangsta," he held up his little hands in the simple pantomime of a gun, and I felt my heart break a little more. This is who they were to him. Instead of a loving birth family that saw to his best interests, they continued to be an example of corruption. In them, he saw an escape from the guilt of misbehavior. Why go to hell when he could just go "home"?

And that's what scared me the most, kept me up at night. This glorification of the "gangsta" lifestyle and mistrust of authority. I feared for him in a world that would read his color before they dared to understand his history. I thought about my baby wanting to go and do "bad things" because of the confusion within him. Already big for his age, I wondered about this same attitude following him into his teen years. No cop would see a frightened child or a kid whose mind had been poisoned against compliance. They wouldn't see a boy with PTSD and a host of other emotional issues, they would see a man-sized child out of control, and shoot him. That was the fear, the anxiety that preyed on me every time he went anywhere near them.

"No baby," I shushed him, pulling him close to me, trying so hard to love this sadness out of him. "Don't say things like that. You're a good boy," I said, kissing his face now streaked with tears. "It's my job to protect you and keep you safe," I continued, the words coming out fast and soft so he wouldn't interrupt me. "I don't ever want you to do bad things, but I'll still love you if you do. Okay?" I kissed his sweet face again, looking deep into eyes that melted my heart and touched my soul. Despite all that we faced, through good times, and it seemed sometimes, an imbalance of bad, he was my baby. He was my baby, and I loved him.

TEXT MESSAGE
FROM MONTAYA

A: GM, can u call Devon

C: After church, of course, I will call Devon

A: I'm waiting

Nvm

I'm sitting on a train track suicidal

CHAPTER 14

Friendtervention

I watched her open cupboard after cupboard in my kitchen. Each fruitless search for whatever she was after, was punctuated by the quiet slam of their doors and the immediate exhale of another opened in its place.

Years of friendship and a bond forged from the fire of shared miseries made her less a guest in my home and more a visiting relative who'd forgotten where the mugs were located.

"Girl, what are you looking for?" I asked, half amused, half irritated by the repeated closing and opening of my cabinet doors.

She turned, twisting her body to face me, arms still outstretched in the continued search. "A plate for all this food I brought," she said absently, returning her body to the task.

Sliding from my perch on a stool at the counter, I walked to where she stood, reaching past her to casually open the cupboard to her left, exposing a mountain of paper plates and other disposable kitchenware.

She snorted a *thank you* in my direction, hands busy pulling plates, forks, bowls, and cups down to the counter. "I'm gonna check on the boys," I called behind me, already on my way up the stairs. She'd brought her son, Mason, over for a playdate and dinner, in part to give the boys some fun time together, but mostly, I felt, to check on me.

I knew I'd been absent. I felt myself a ghost, haunting the life I used to live while still adjusting to my new existence "on the other side," wondering how to make substantial contact with those left behind. I was grateful for Claudia, a friend determined to not let me fade away completely.

The unseen hand of motherhood, at times, cradled me, tethered me, held my own weak hand as I fought battles I never dreamed I'd be on the front lines of. On other occasions, it pushed me toward an exhaustion I could, at times, scarcely survive and pulled me away from the help and care I was loathe to admit I needed.

I rounded the corner at the top of my stairs and strained to hear beyond the beeps and bloops of some video game the boys were smack talking their way through. Peeking into his game room, I saw my son, criss-cross applesauce as he'd been taught by so many different institutions, enjoying the company of his friend. His pink tongue hanging out of his slightly open mouth, determination etched into every line of his chubby little face. I felt some relief, the normalcy of it all causing me to sag against the wall in gratitude. We could be any other family, I thought to myself. Montaya and the stress she introduced to our lives on a near constant basis seemed so far away when viewed under the glow of a game console monitor. I left them to it and made my way back downstairs to offer help I knew would be refused.

"How they doin'?" Claudia asked, her back to me as she rotated various Tupperware bowls in and out of the microwave with the ease and confidence of a woman who knew exactly what she was doing and had done it many times.

"Quiet," I was happy to report, dropping the tired weight of my body back into a chair.

"What about you?" She stilled her endless rotation for a moment, spinning so her back rested against the counter, arms bent back at the elbows ready to launch her to my aid.

"I'm fine." It was my standard answer. "I'm fine," I would say with a shrug and well-crafted half-smile. "Fine," was the mask I wore. "Fine," was a mantra I said over and over, a word of strength and indifference used to conceal the fact that I was anything but.

"I know," she said. "I know you're 'fine.' I know you don't need any help, with anything, ever. But girl, you don't look good. When's the last time you got your hair done, went to the gym, did anything for yourself? You still deserve to do those things, you know that right?" Her mouth, usually wide in a smile or open in laughter, was now turned down at the corners, lines etched deeply on either side.

She was right. I knew she was. The stress of Devon's everyday care overwhelmed me, consumed me, and in the midst of that most important work, I was losing a bit of myself. I no longer had time for the things I found so important before motherhood. Getting to the gym, keeping myself in shape, caring enough to fill in the cracks.

"I know," I said simply, not able to fake away the weariness I felt. I looked at Claudia and thought of the sometimes harsh, but honest friendship we enjoyed. If not for her, I might never have opened myself up enough to let the Lord bless me with a child. When Brian walked away, it was she who attended classes with me to ready me for this amazing journey. Of all my friends, I valued her support the most. She wasn't just handing out platitudes, congratulating me on being such a good person for taking care of my child, she lived it, walked it, knew the world I'd entered like the back of her hand.

I'd met her a several years earlier at work. It was rare to find another woman in my field with the same cultural background, with so much in common with myself. Women in the workplace can be so toxic, so unrelentingly petty, it had long been my policy to focus on work and forge my personal relationships elsewhere. Claudia was different.

I felt I knew her and, more importantly, she knew me. She wasn't a rival or a professional liability, she was a kindred. Our shared memories of growing up in the Midwest created a bond between us that went from mere acquaintanceship to sisterhood. Having worked for the same consulting company, we made our move to Charlotte not together, but near enough around the same time, it seemed we were nearly fated to be friends. Our love of culture and people found us going out together often, and I grew to love her.

Claudia's no-nonsense attitude reminded me so much of my own, and I appreciated her sincerity. She met me when I was still very much invested in the habits and peculiarities of being a Mrs. to a man that had never once deserved to be my Mr., and I think she saw in me, a bit of her own struggle. We both tried so hard to legitimize relationships that were clearly unequally yoked, loving men that hated us for shouldering the financial burdens they created.

When it became clear my efforts to conceive would not and could not bear fruit, it was under Claudia's guidance that I began to explore the option of fostering. Her savvy and experience: stemming from the guardianship of her sister's children, gave me a sense of reassurance. Someone had been here before me, and it was all right.

"You can't keep doing this," she said, snatching me out of my reverie. "You've got to cut these people loose."

I knew "the people" she meant: Devon's parents, "The Biologicals" as I had taken to calling them.

I was sick of hearing it, really. I was sick of people looking at my situation from a surface perspective and then deciding with such certainty what I "needed" to do. No one knew what was at stake for him, or for me. No one knew what I had invested, but absolutely everyone had the answers to questions I wasn't asking.

"And then what?" I asked, more than a hint of edge to my voice, my spine a little straighter, my eyes now narrowed. "I cut them loose, and then what?"

"You know it can't go on like this," she said quietly, brown hair rippling at her shoulders as she shook her head at me. "I wish you could see what I see. You hardly ever smile anymore, Carla. Do you know that? That such a happy thing should bring you so much sorrow, certainly says something, in my personal opinion. And the way you play victim," she shook her head again, though now it seemed in disgust, "the woman I met a few years back would never behave this way, would never let these people defeat her the way you let them defeat you."

"You don't understand," I interjected, angry now. This was another one of my well-used and most treasured phrases, employed to put people back in their place and protect me from their judgment. I didn't invite her over to hear this nor did I invite her over to be told what I was doing wrong in the midst of all I was trying to do right.

"I do understand!" her voice loud in the quiet of my kitchen. The microwave beeped its alert, interrupting our tense exchange long enough for Claudia to return to her task. Wanting to appear busy as well, I swiveled my body up and out of my barstool to collect the plates and cutlery she'd left on the counter.

"We all understand," she said after a time, clearly wanting to choose her words carefully. She didn't look at me, didn't look up at all in fact, but continued to move hot food from hot Tupperware, to cool platters, to the empty table. "We do understand, and we know you love Devon, and that'd you do anything for him." The straightforwardness that I so enjoyed about her could often be tough to take when turned on me, but I listened.

"Is that wrong, though?" I asked, "Is it wrong for me to fight for him?" I asked with as withering an accusation as I could muster. "I'm trying to save his life, Claudia. I'm his mother."

"No," she said gravely, delicately balancing a pitcher of water in one hand and a bowl of dinner rolls in the other. "Montaya is his mother, and you're the woman that can't let him go."

I felt my chest nearly collapse at my sudden intake of air. The anger I felt prickling hot and fast on my skin moved up my throat and out of my mouth before I could slow the dangerous speed of its arrival. "How dare you -- you say something like that to me!" I hissed incredulously. "You will never know, never know what I do for that child, what I--"

"Yeah, I do know," she cut me off, "but what I want to know is who asked you to, and how much longer you're going to let it go on? Who asked you to sacrifice your whole life for this child? Who told you that you had a right to take him away from his mother? Who told you that you were right?" she went on, the dinner forgotten for now, steam rolling up absently from the table between us. "When I met you, you were so full of life, so funny, so *together*," she clenched her hand now in a fist, I guess in an effort to demonstrate just how "together" past me was. "You used to be the most interesting woman in the room, and now, this is the only story you have to tell. We all see the game she's playing. Why can't you?"

"Devon's life is not a game," I said stiffly, not sure what more, if anything I could say.

"No it's not," she agreed with me, her voice softening. "So imagine how confusing it must be for him to be tugged between these two worlds. What do you think it does to him to come here and then have to go home-- yes, his home," she insisted, predicting an argument from me. "These people are using you, using that baby as a stronghold over your life until there is nothing left for them to take. Montaya knows your pay schedule and how much you love the one thing she has that you don't. Do you have any idea how dangerous that makes her and how vulnerable it makes you? I can't be silent anymore. I can't watch you destroy yourself for these people. I know who they are. My sister tried to put me through this same mess, thinking she had the upper hand, but you cannot rationalize with these people. What is common and regular to them is not the same for us, and you need to stop waiting and expecting for everything to just fall into place. It is never going to be like that." The last word came out as thin and weak as a ghost.

"This food is getting cold," I said after a moment, willing my anger and frustration to settle. "I'll go get *our* boys," I said, walking up the stairs without another word.

CHAPTER 15

The Attack

"Turn this motherfucking car around!" That's Montaya, her voice shaking through the interior of my car with venom. Montaya, her voice dripping with an almost disgusted impatience. She was mad about something, probably money, and Devon was in the back seat: silent, watchful.

I see us in the car, our mouths working, eyebrows furrowed in anger. But what about, I don't know. I'm experiencing the scene in bursts, like static from a tv with a loose antenna. I can see the picture, but the resolution is off. I can only intuit that something is different, and I'm powerless to change the channel.

I see Montaya raise her hand, quicker than I've ever seen her move, and feel the force of her backhand mashing my lips against my teeth before I've even registered what she'd done. Though I'm driving, I see us look at each other in horror and surprise, our expressions reflections of one another.

Oh my God, you hit me

Oh, my God, I hit you

We're locked in the truth of our relationship now, and with the eyes of my soul, I see us both acknowledge that change is on the horizon. We cannot continue on from here. I can no longer be the abused. I can no longer be the enabler.

"Miss Carla, I'm sorry!" she says to me from what feels a great distance. Her features, warped by tears I cannot stop, seem contrite. I know we have someplace to be, but a feeling, hot and prickly up and down the surface of my skin, urges me to pull over. I'm too stunned to drive any further.

I still haven't spoken, as I'm not quite sure what to say. I don't know whether to fight or flee, but I feel strongly that I need to leave the car. The car isn't safe. I'm not safe.

I'm not safe.

It's the first time I've really let the thought sink into my brain. Every day that I'm with these people, I am putting myself and my child in danger. *I am not safe.*

I can't help the tears that find their way down my cheeks. The anger, humiliation, and fear associated with being slapped like a child in front of my son digs into my soul with heat, with shame. No wonder he didn't respect me. Through my passivity, I'd taught him that love and compassion were weaknesses easily slapped down by the person with the loudest voice.

"He didn't see nothing Miss. Carla," Montaya insisted as I unsnapped my seatbelt, fumbling with the door handle, needing to get out of the car. "He didn't see, he don't know," she repeated, chirping like a bird at dawn. I could hear the fear in her voice. A woman that lived to push boundaries and bully others to get her way, understood that she'd overstepped. With each passing minute, her hold on me was slipping, and though I'm sure it wasn't her intention, that slap woke me up.

I stepped out of the car, the driver's side door shut firmly behind me, and I dropped to my knees. I didn't know what else to do. I had done everything, had tried everything, and I was lost.

Please.

I prayed silently, tears running down my bruised cheeks and swollen lip.

Lord, please.

And there, in the parking lot of a store I can't remember, I gave up.

PRINTOUT OF VOICE MESSAGE FROM MONTAYA

Please call me asap wreak car yesterday I'm so sad u promise not to do dis I'm so sorry that I cross u please forgive me I'm lost

CHAPTER 16

Three Days

After the attack, my focus began immediately to change. It was as if the feel of her flesh against my face opened up a reserve of resolve in me, and I knew it was long past time to get us out. Several events had unfolded in the wake of that smack, and I understood my time was running out.

Since the attack, Devon's considerable emotional challenges, when put up against the death of a family friend, spiraled into the nightmare of attempted suicide: twice, in fact. In what universe did a six-year-old child have such sadness inside them, they wanted to end their own life? Further, where did a six-year-old even learn suicide as a coping mechanism? My baby, tormented by so much confusion and hurt in his little life, ran from school, into oncoming traffic, to cancel the darkness inside him. How serious the actual attempt was, I cannot say. At six, I'm not positive he could possibly understand the weight of such a decision, but if I didn't regard his attempt as the final zero on a slow-moving countdown clock, then I was failing him.

What can I do? Turned to *I have to do something*, and I felt safety in the transition.

I had spent so much time figuring out how to make *them* comfortable enough to allow me to stay in Devon's life. My energy, time, and money were spent saying "yes," for fear that a "no" would banish me from his world forever, and in so doing, I'd made prisoners of us both. Because I could not bear to lose him, I'd failed to realize how much I never actually had him. I'd come to realize that being a mother was more than midnight feedings, and bath times, and cuddles. Motherhood, I'd finally come to understand, was really about protection.

Yes, I had to do something, but what, in fact, *could* I do? I'd been stuck in neutral for so long, idling as this woman and her ilk terrorized us from the comfort of a life I'd subsidized, that now, ready to put my life in drive, I had no concept of direction. The system that I'd trusted to take care of him, look out for him, acted on the discretion of its judges to put him deeper and deeper in harm's way, and as a result, I was reluctant to lean on their involvement.

Suggestions in every shape and color came from my friends and family. "Let it go," was the of-quoted piece of advice, and while I understood, I wasn't quite there. How could I "let it go?" What was the expectation there, I wondered? I would just, what? Tally my losses, shrug my shoulders, and leave him in the hands of people hell-bent on destroying everything good in him? No matter how many times I heard it, I simply could not do that. I would never do that.

The logical answer, of course, was to call child protective services. Montaya had told me more than once that she'd kill Devon before she let "them" take him away. Obviously, if I alerted the authorities of the threat to Devon's life, they would remove him from the home, at least temporarily, until something more permanent could be worked out. And while that maneuver felt like a good one, I knew if I involved

DSS, Montaya could also request that I never see him again, and what access I had would be stripped away indefinitely. Though this solution took him safely out of their poisonous reach, he would be forever out of mine, as well. Spite and vindictiveness grew from her like bitter fruit from a rotten tree, and though it would ultimately hurt Devon, she would succeed in hurting me, righting the mantle of power once more.

The very thought of it killed me, thinking of him growing up without me. I pictured, with an anguished heart, him learning to call someone else "mommy," and someone usurping all the love I'd put into him. My soul screamed at such a notion, but my baby would be free, and that was enough to quiet the ache in my heart when it came right down to it.

"Commit her," my niece-in-love said, matter-of-factly, with support from my sister. "A 72-hour hold would be more than enough time to convince the proper authorities that Devon is in danger in that house." My niece-in-love, wife to my sweet nephew, had worked in mental health long enough to know what she was talking about, and I trusted her knowledge. The question of what to do with Devon had become a matter of family discussion, and I was so grateful for the support. For too long I'd hidden the reality of our lives away for fear of what others might think or say. The time for those fears was over, and I let my family in.

"No." I wasn't sure why, but the idea unsettled my spirit. On paper, it was sound. Contain Montaya long enough to save Devon. And while it seemed a good plan, it seemed not to be a good solution. To me, it was like putting a band-aid over a wound far too infected to heal conventionally. Instead of acting on the advice of my loved-ones, I prayed, and I waited instead. I waited for the Lord to show me the correct path, to show me how I could save my baby. I knew the only way to truly break the cycle, was to remove him from that home "period" and by any means at my disposal, within the stiflingly tight quarters of the law.

In the wake of my six year old's second suicide attempt, time was running out, and the waiting was hard. How many more attempts? How many more sleepless nights, trips to the hospital, and sessions with behavioral health could my 1st grader withstand before my efforts to save him from himself also failed? I needed him safe, but also, I just needed him to be okay. I needed him to be able to conquer the demons of his childhood so he could grow and prosper into the man I saw he could become. The last six years felt like a battle between good and evil. And in my refusal to let the darkness beat out the light, I felt paralyzed. In that stillness, I'd learned to be patient, knowing that battles are fought and won with time and grace. So I waited, and as I waited, several events began to unfold that let me know the Lord will always answer, if we're quiet enough to listen. In the midst of this turmoil, three days were absolutely critical in determining the direction we could safely go -- three days -- which brought clarity, answers, and, ultimately, a way out for Devon and me both.

Long ago, my estate planning attorney had given me the name of three law firms that specialized in family law who might be able to help me. And the time had come, I felt, to finally ask for some help.

I needed help.

October 24th, I contacted the first of three attorneys on the list given to me and simply hoped. That same day, Devon's dad dismissed the therapy "our" son so desperately needed and refused in home-therapy. This act, coupled with the twin offenses of Montaya attacking me in the car, the repeated making threats against me and

Devon's life was the final bit of motivation I needed to move forward, no holds barred. I was tired of conceding to their ignorance and folly. I was sick of sacrificing his well-being to make them happy, and if I lost him, so be it. I felt, at last, strong enough to bear the pain of his absence if it meant he was safe somewhere without them. Once I accepted that simple truth into my heart, an entire world opened up before me. I was his mother. I would protect him.

That first name on the list was of absolutely no help to me, and with a heart heavily shadowed by doubt, I pressed on toward the second, determined to get us the help we needed.

"....Law Offices," said a crisp, but helpful, voice on the other end of the line. Though initially, I'd planned only to state my name and contact information when instructed to do so, I felt myself instead unearthing six years of truth into that woman's ear. I told her of my fears, my concerns, and ultimately my objective: get him out.

"Hold the line ma'am," she said to me, and my heart sighed at the words. She didn't say, "I'll have someone get back to you." No, "I'm sorry, our client list is currently full." She said none of the things I was prepared to hear and gave me the one thing for which I had not been prepared: hope. The third firm I called was different. I spoke with the paralegal and later that same day, I had the chance to speak with the attorney for that firm as well. He was amazing.

That one conversation changed everything, and the very next day, October 25th, I was walking into that same law firm and signed papers to be represented in a move to gain emergency protective custody of my son. After that, things moved more quickly than I could have imagined. I had representation, and I had a plan, which is more than I'd had since the start of this horrific journey, and though

I could ill afford to rest easy, I could feel the grip of fear relax ever so slightly.

I liked my lawyer, which isn't vital, but I did find it helpful. His blue eyes were sharp, and his fine, strawberry-blonde hair made him look trustworthy and approachable. He didn't have the strident, dour visage of the court as I had come to know it. Instead of turning me away at the door, as I had expected, he looked eager to take me on -- if only for the sake of the challenge.

Finding the right representation was the key I'd been missing. In all my years of struggle against a system I felt truly did not represent the interests of either my child or myself, I found refuge within its jargon and statutes. Within a day, my counsel felt I had sufficient grounds to move forward with an Ex-parte protection order, which in emergency situations was good for ten days. And just like that, I was able to do, in three days, what I had not been able to in six years.

"And after ten days?" I asked. Sure, ten days was a victory, but I needed to make sure he would not return to that house.

"*In loco parentis,*" my lawyer said to me simply, waiting for the words to sink in.

"What is that?" I answered, not sure how more Latin was the answer to my question. Buoyed by the plan we'd set into motion, I could not rid myself of the anxiety I felt. I had trusted in the system once, and it crushed me, utterly defeated me. I was no longer in the mood for the misleading semantics of the law. I wanted answers that I could trust and understand, not more legal loopholes that allowed for the continued exploitation of my vulnerability.

"*In loco parentis,*" he repeated, drawing his chair closer to the big mahogany desk between us. "It literally translates to 'in place of parent,' based on a long-standing statute. Basically," he continued, long hands moving expressively, eager to explain how this might help us, "under certain circumstances it can allow for a non-biological parent to be given the legal rights and responsibilities of a biological parent if they have acted as a parent for a significant amount of time in the child's life. You've never heard this?" He asked, incredulously, looking as surprised as I felt.

I sat back in my chair, flabbergasted. I thought of the thousands of dollars, from my own pocket, that I'd spent on Devon's health, nutrition, safety, and general everyday needs over the course of his six years on earth. I thought of the battles I fought for his mental health and access to quality education and had to laugh. *In loco parentis.* The words had weight, held promise, and this was the first time I had ever heard them. Not one person had ever mentioned it -- not social workers, DSS, the child advocacy groups, the attorneys I had consulted, and not the whole flawed system that dragged him back into hell. The ignorance of the system and their willingness to let a child suffer over semantics blew my mind, and in addition to being resolved, I was angry.

"Now what we need," he said thoughtfully, fingers steepled over the leather blotter on his desk, "is evidence. We need to make a case for the danger you perceive him to be in, as well as a case for your fitness as a parent over theirs: receipts, records, anything at all would be helpful in a case like this. Do you have anything like that?"

Smiling, I produced a thick manila file from my bag.

CHAPTER 17

Court Begins

With an ex-parte order, we were not required to notify "the parents," due to the emergency status of the situation, and I sought to enact immediately. Paired with restraining orders against both of the biological parents to discourage all contact with Devon or myself during the ten-day window, I let myself breathe, just a little bit.

With the help of my lawyer and his truly thorough paralegal, we built a case that was both strong, and in my opinion, irrefutable. In reviewing the facts of the case three things were clear:

1. Montaya and Wayne, the defendants, are unfit to parent Devon.

2. The defendants have neglected Devon's welfare and interests.

3. The defendants have acted in a manner inconsistent with their constitutionally protected status.

Seeing it there, in black and white, finally gave me the confidence I'd been lacking. I'd been hopeful that things would work out in our favor, but to see our struggle laid out in scribbles on legal pads, and notarized on 8 ½ x 11 sheets of paper, made victory a bit more tangible. No longer would I be a slave, an ATM, a patsy to do their bidding while begging for scraps of Devon's life. No longer did I have to lie awake, my stomach in knots, worrying about what he'd eaten for dinner, or if he was sleeping on clean sheets. And no longer would my baby be a pawn -- a toy for them to manipulate and control to produce whatever outcome they wanted. He was home, and I finally had the right weapons in my arsenal to keep him there. Ten days wasn't long, but it was a start.

Court was ridiculous. Montaya and Wayne would show up belligerent, ignorant, and wholly unprepared to fight for the child they insisted they had a right to. Wayne, for all his nonsensical swagger, threatened me within the walls of the courtroom itself, promising to "bust my head to the white meat," undaunted by the ears that heard or the eyes that saw him do it.

Their antics would have been enough to frustrate any judge, I think. But in addition to their behavior, every single day of the last six years damned them in a court of law. In the eyes of the court, they had turned over all child-raising and decision-making responsibilities for Devon, to me. Take-backs weren't going to work here.

The motion for custody was granted.

Outside of court, their heckling and harassment became relentless. I endured call after call, threats of every conceivable nature, text messages, and the harassment of my friends as well. Montaya published my name and address to her social media, putting out an "all call" for anybody wanting to "take care of me" for her. They blustered and brayed, but I continued. I'd been through hell with these people. What were a few threatening phone calls to me? Each call or attempt to contact me was in direct violation of the Domestic Violence Order of Protection I had against each of them. During this time they were arrested for these violations, and I prayed they would eventually just let us be.

Though I wasn't scared of Montaya and Wayne, I was concerned for the general safety and well-being of Devon, and obviously myself. I did what I could, short of moving out of my house. I alerted our neighbors, alerted his school, and installed a four-camera security system for my property. From there, all I could do was wait for the courts to catch up with my heart and legally make us a family.

EXCERPT

Order For Temporary Custody

BASED UPON THE FOREGOING FINDINGS OF FACT, THE COURT MAKES THE FOLLOWING:

CONCLUSIONS OF LAW

IT IS THEREFORE ORDERED AS FOLLOWS:

1. Plaintiff, CARLA__, is granted sole temporary custody of the minor child, Devon, born____.

2. Defendants shall not remove or attempt to remove the minor child from the custody of Plaintiff, school, from any of the child's medical providers, or from anyone whom Plaintiff has chosen to provide childcare, pending further Order of the Court.

3. Plaintiff is a fit and proper person to assume the parenting role set forth herein.

CHAPTER 18

With Eviction Comes Reality

The issue of custody now settled, at least temporarily, my next order of business focused squarely on getting Devon's parents out of my house. It became my mission, in the quest to secure the safety and stability of my son, that any and all ties to his biological parents be severed completely. And, by the way, I couldn't enter my own property due to the restraining orders as long as they lived there.

I filed a motion to evict them from the property I'd purchased for their use, and with a sense of cooperation I was now coming to respect from the North Carolina court system, it was granted and put into motion. I wanted to ensure the safety of my property during what was sure to be a stressful transition and employed the help of a friend in hiding cameras around the property to make sure no further damage would be done.

In the wake of their leaving, I believe I was more crushed than angry. They had literally destroyed my property, turned it into their own private playpen, so sure someone would be along to clean up their mess. I walked through the piles of garbage, so thick you could barely see the floor, and tried to imagine my son ever playing there. I looked at the sink, basins stacked with weeks-worth of dishes and pictured what dinner time must have been like for him.

The refrigerator held no pictures, no artwork to mark his passage through school; its contents empty of any food, nutritious or otherwise. The house smelled stale, rotten, and neglected. I felt myself grow angry, but really, who was I mad at? Them, for being and acting exactly as expected? Or me, for stupidly believing they would do anything but?

All-in-all, my clean-up crew collected over fifteen bags of trash, and I paid thousands of dollars in repairs and damages to fix the house.

In addition to the containers of spoiled food, mountains of clothing, a slop jar, and mattresses so black with filth it would have been better to burn them, the lawn crew found two guns hidden inside a tree on the property, three bags of crack, burnt spoons, cans (to make crack pipes) and a few needles as well. Whether I chose to admit or not, whether I had been complicit or not, in trying to keep my baby, I had been financing a crack house. Shaking my head, I towed my son's broken toys out of the way, and continued silently down the hall.

TEXT MESSAGE FROM MONTAYA

I've reach out to attorney no
Response I'm bout to go
Crazy haven't see u or Devon
Such OCT 24 I understand ure

protecting Devon Carla but all we
had to do was talk over I love u
as my mom never meant no harm
and u promise never too throw me out

or take Devon away from me or
put me in jail I'm saying this just this just
in case u try lock me up again

are u seriously DAT desperate for our child
Devon is a part of us all u can stop this restrictions against us and
let's us be a family again please
Carla I'm sorry

CHAPTER 19

The Book of Parenting

"Look at my son." I sat relaxed against the cushions of my sofa, looking at him with equal parts disappointment and sadness. "Look at my son, as handsome as he is, acting straight up like he doesn't know any better when I know that he does," I continued, trying hard to reinforce our mother-son bond; trying hard to remind him of who I was raising him to be.

"Fuck you, bitch!" he screamed, followed by a shockingly childish raspberry, spit clinging to his sullen lower lip, sliding down his dark, angry chin.

As always, it was difficult to hear such ugliness come out of his handsome little face. He stared at me with his nostrils flared and his strong brown hands curled into angry fists. Graham crackers littered the gray tile floor, cinnamon-scented casualties in a war fought all too often.

Devon was mad at me.

"Don't talk like that, baby." I sat, impassive on the brown leather sectional, reflecting on the same basic formula that led us here every day. I pondered the equation and wondered which variables I could tweak to produce a different outcome or at least stumble on a new solution that resulted in fewer graham crackers on my floor. It was simple, really: Devon, plus an unsatisfied desire, equaled an immediate meltdown. Today's unsatisfied desire came in the form of sweets I wouldn't allow him to eat before dinner. Though this rule was long established, and despite its obvious logic, Devon's response remained the same. He wanted the graham crackers, therefore, he should have the graham crackers. Any course of action in opposition to receiving the desired "thing," was met with violence and disrespect. These episodes lasted until I yielded or he was exhausted, and they were every day, several times a day.

"Look at my son," I tried again, unfazed by the vulgarity that had long lost its shock value, I pressed forward, "the son I'm so proud of and who I love so much." I stared back at him from my position on the couch, refusing to react. This behavior was so much like Montaya that it almost made me sad. This was the most recognizable evidence of her involvement in his life for the past 6 years or so: these frightening bursts of anger that consumed every ounce of my energy and peace. It was during these moments of rage that I flashed forward to a future where all authority in Devon's life was met with this same violent defiance, and I quaked in fear for him. What kind of life could my baby ever hope to have? What would be his response when his teacher, principal, or coach asked him to do something he didn't like? I envisioned a world of endless parent/teacher conferences, suspensions, or God forbid, expulsions. What sort of job or success could he ever possibly achieve, when every demand made of him received a "fuck you," in response? Lastly, what would happen to my sweet son if a broken tail-light or missed stop sign ever caused him to be pulled over? Would a cop stop and look into his eyes and see the gentle child that I raised? A boy that likes football, and pretty girls, and Uno? Or, would a cop take one look at his brown skin and defiant stance, and then decide his life doesn't matter? These thoughts and others dominated me during these moments. Could I repair what his parents tried so hard to break before it was too late?

"Do you think it's nice to talk like that to mommy?" I asked without emotion. Just as I had had to learn with his mother, I made myself as neutral as possible during these dark times in hopes that he would follow my lead out of these dark places.

"Shut up, before I hit you in your muh'fuckin eye!" He screamed, flipping a chair as he did so, demonstrating that he would absolutely carry out his threat if I did not, in fact, shut up. I took in his size and felt the warning of his threat. Big for his age, my lovable six-year-old was built like a ten-year-old, and when angry, had the strength of a teenager. In the midst of these storms, sometimes all I could do was hold him down, his arms pinned safely to his side before he could hurt me or himself. More than anything, in these moments, my heart ached. Would he ever be able to overcome the damage done to him?

I could only shake my head. All of it: the cursing, the yelling, the physical aggression, were soiled pages torn straight from the Montaya-and-Wayne-book-of-parenting. I don't believe a day went by without a "fuck you," "you ain' shit," "bitch," or some threat of violence in that house while he was there. My baby and I were two sad actors, forever on stage, reading from the same poorly written script. I worried every day for my baby. Already so big for his age, I obsessed anxiously over a day a police officer, someone looking for a fight, or someone just afraid of his skin and his size, asked him to do something he didn't like. What then? If I couldn't teach him a better way, what then?

"I love you no matter what." He looked up at me sharply, the whites of his eyes nearly blue in their purity, widened around his shocked brown pupils. "Do you even know why you're angry?" I investigated further, wanting to take advantage of his full attention.

"Yes," he whispered softly, giving his leg a light but determined punch. "You won't let me have my game." He stood there, looking small and powerless in his rumpled khakis and sky blue school polo.

"That's right," I nodded sagely, letting it sink in. "And why won't I let you have your game?" I wanted him to verbalize his behavior, to say it out loud so we could examine it together.

His fist came down again, harder this time, with more intention to harm. "Don't do that," I chided, not wanting him to hurt himself. "Put your hands on your knees, Devon. Come on, tell me why I won't let you use your electronics." His head shook slowly, shame adding weight to his movements. He knew better. I could see it.

A trauma victim from birth, Devon suffered from PTSD, DMDD, ADHD, anxiety and depression, and host of other letter combinations which left my son a moody, anger-prone, and all around combative force of nature when confronted with the notion of not getting his way. Along with the screaming, cursing, throwing things, and acting out physically, he would also lapse into self-harm if he felt the aforementioned tactics weren't working. Picking his nose enough to make it bleed or gouging scratches deep into his skin were merely more tricks of the trade. If his biological mother had taught him anything, it was this: if anger and violence won't get you your way, then sympathy surely will.

"BECAUSE YOU GET ON MY NERVES! Bitch!" He answered finally, clearly tired of my efforts to calm him down. The language and disrespect were tools of aggression parroted from his parents. In my baby's world, authority sounded like vulgarity. You got people to do what you wanted by threatening and belittling them. Montaya got Wayne to cook her meals, fetch her drink, clean up after her, by screaming at him, by insulting him into submission. Wayne, in turn, let Montaya know exactly how he felt about it, by calling her a "no good bitch," at every given opportunity.

Devon, I said his full name firmly, irritation now making my voice tight. I loved this child with the entirety of my heart, but I was getting pissed. We'd smoothly moved into the "destroy things" phase of today's third tantrum and as his fist raised to crash down on my end table, I'd had enough. "You better not!" I raised my voice over the din of his rage. "Go to time out right now and put your hands on your knees!" The directions were supposed to be simple enough to follow without discussion and gave him a task on which to focus in order to bring him out of his anger.

"No!" He screamed back in a just as simple but direct response, his fist finally connecting with the wooden table, sending batteries, remotes, magazines, and Kleenex crashing to the floor as I sprang to my feet.

"Go to time out and put your hands on your knees," I pointed to the camouflage bean bag chair against the wall of my living room. "No electronics for the rest of the night if you don't get yourself under control right now." My own nostrils flared, tired beyond measure, I stared at him until he understood there'd be no concession from me.

Having now clearly moved beyond graham crackers, he drew back his arm, meaty little fist cocked and ready, and bucked his body in my direction. A smugness tamed his curled upper lip into a genuinely upsetting smile when I took a flinching step backward. "See, that's why you scared. Don't make me hit you in the face like my mama did."

Ignoring the bait, for now, I repeated my request and waited patiently for compliance, relieved, perhaps more than I wanted to admit when he turned and threw himself onto the timeout bean bag. Its misshapen form, due more to abuse than an abundance of beans, it now held the angry weight of a child spent and sullen. His beautiful eyes wild and staring, I watched him place his hands on his knees as I'd asked, but not before turning his fingers into two brown birds, the middle fingers jutting up like malevolent skyscrapers in a run-down city.

It had been months since Devon had seen either Montaya or Wayne, and I knew their continued absence confused him. What could I say? Other than, "your mom and dad need to work on themselves before they can take care of you;" how could I talk him out of missing people who had only said the words "I love you," but had never shown it with their actions? The violence and anger he displayed more and more, I knew were his way of articulating a fear that he'd never see his mom and dad again. I think he knew, whether he could understand it yet or not, that they would never get themselves together.

CHAPTER 20

Victim or Victimizer

M ontaya,
I want to hate her. Despite what I've been taught, despite what I hear from the pulpit on Sundays, my heart wants to hate her.

But that same heart knows the truth: she can't help but be Montaya.

She'd told me about the sexual abuse she suffered at the hands of her father, and discussed with a matter-of-fact-air, how her mother would often pimp her for drugs. I looked at this woman, whose chances for salvation were so few and, try as I might, my pity for her far outweighed my antipathy.

In Montaya's world, children were possessions, a token you received in the game of life that proved someone loved you. Much like property, you could really never have enough, and it didn't matter what you did with it; it was yours.

Don't make me hit you in the face like my momma did.

Though I'd ignored it initially, the statement upset me more than I let on. I thought back to that day, remembering even now the shock of her hand on my skin and all it had set into motion. She'd assured me that Devon hadn't seen what she'd done, but I knew better. And hadn't I been right? What didn't those big eyes see?

There's so little consolation in having our worst fears confirmed.

My very bones ached as I arched my body up from the couch. In this way, I felt very connected to the other mothers I knew. Motherhood had changed my body in ways I did not expect, but felt every day. I'd always prided myself on my toned physique and enjoyment of physical activity, but with motherhood always comes sacrifice, and I now felt my age and exhaustion in every inch of softening flesh. And though silvery stretch marks didn't circle the childless circumference of my belly, surely the stretch marks around my heart had to count for something.

Dragging myself to the kitchen, I opened the refrigerator, instinctively throwing up a hand to stay the avalanche of take-out containers and Tupperware fruit chunks angling to escape. My mind was thick, crowded with images, colors, and just so much noise as I prepared myself a glass of lemon water. Something about the simple mechanics of its preparation soothed me. Cut the lemon, juice it, drop it in the infuser, drink it, feel better. As I took my first nourishing gulp, I let it slide down into my stomach, willing it to detoxify not only my body but my clogged spirit as well.

Hit you like my momma did

The phrase stayed with me as I shuffled, tired legs and all, back to the couch. Bedtime had drained me, as it quite often did. Though we eventually settled The Great Graham Cracker Debate, the path to victory had been hard-fought on both sides. I was happy that Devon could drift into calm, un-agitated sleep, but I was not so blessed. He'd wake up tomorrow, fresh for another battle, the impact of this last skirmish all but erased from his memory. Me? I drew this withering exchange, and so many others like it, onto the scarred and crowded walls of my heart.

The tv murmured, merely acting as company while I sat alone in my living room. The graham crackers had been begrudgingly swept up and thrown away, a faint hint of spice lingered in their absence.

Like my momma did

The words shimmered in front of me, blinked on and off like a neon sign above a door I never again wanted to walk through. Even now, trying as I might to step past it on the edge of my thoughts, the memory itself seemed hazy, ephemeral. I know there was an argument that day, but about what I can't remember. In truth, it could have been about anything. Montaya didn't need an excuse to be angry; her very existence served as justification enough. The entire scene, as I reflected upon it, came to me in black and white. Soundless, the images around us are sped up, jerky almost, but Montaya and I are squarely in the middle, a tableau, motionless amongst the chaos.

I'm grateful, if not for the slap, then the jarring call back to reality. Who's to say how much longer I would have let us dangle in her web? In the comfort of my home, a thing she had never really had, I could look at the pile of ashes from which God had delivered me, with praise on my lips and joy in my heart. Yes, there would be struggles. Tonight's tantrum wouldn't be the last, but I also knew with patience, the correct resources, and the love I was made to give him, Devon would get what he needed to overcome the issues plaguing us now, and his future was as bright and open as any other child's. I believe that.

So many people in my life have remarked upon the fantastic luck responsible for bringing Devon and me together. "He's so *lucky* to have found you, Carla," I often heard, and accepted with gritted teeth. I smiled through my irritation and bowed my head in humble thanks for the compliment, but the truth of the matter was: *I was lucky. I was blessed to have found him.* Devon saved me, and whatever problems lay before us, I knew they could never be as frightening as the ones that lay behind. No matter what else we were to face, I knew only one truth:

I was his mother, and he was my son.

EXCERPT

<u>Order for Permanent Custody</u>

BASED UPON THE FOREGOING FINDINGS OF FACT, THE COURT MAKES THE FOLLOWING:

3. Plaintiff is a fit and proper person to assume the parenting role set forth herein.

8. It would be in the best interest of Devon for Plaintiff to be granted his sole care, custody, and control.

9. It would be in the best interest of Devon, for the Defendants to have no contact with Devon.

IT IS THEREFORE ORDERED AS FOLLOWS:

1. Plaintiff, Carla___, is granted sole custody of the minor child, Devon _____.

CHAPTER 21
A New Beginning

"Are you ready?" My sister asks, bringing me sharply back to the present as we wait outside the courtroom. I wasn't sure how long I'd been sitting there, silent, worrying over the day's monumental tasks and outcome. "Just a little bit longer, and it's all over," she smiles at me reassuringly, voice full of love and concern, her hands cool and dry as she grips me. She is so eager to comfort me, to introduce some calm to combat my nerves, but I've fought the battle long enough to not get my hopes too far up. We're closer than we were, but I can never afford to think that it will ever be "over."

Today is an important day. While not the last step, it's the first in a remaining few that will sever the ties between my baby and the birth parents who brought him into the world. And depending on so many factors, I will be one step closer to the dream I've held in my heart since the moment I laid eyes on him: adoption.

"I'm ready," my smile lies back to her. I don't know why, but my stomach has been a riot of nerves since the moment I woke up. I'd spent the previous night preparing and though nearly every moment of the last eight years has come down to this moment, I'm nervous and ill at ease. While things, for the moment, were indeed going our way-- there had been some bumps.

Shaking my head, I take a moment to reflect on how funny life can and will often be. My mouth quirks in a grim smile as I think once again of the judge presiding over today's hearing. Though before the termination of parental rights hearing began, I had never met her personally, I had certainly seen her name before. I think my mind has worked very hard to suppress it, as it often tries to do with unpleasantness. Back then, she was no more than a signature on a page, a ghost I could neither fight nor question. Today, she was the honorable judge presiding over the hearing that could change every-thing. Eight years ago, she was the judge that took my baby away.

Looking down at the court papers clutched in my hand, I'm in disbelief. How can this be? How could something like this ever happen? I feel like the air has been punched from my stomach. Just how hard was it supposed to be?

"This has got to be a conflict of interest," I seethed between clenched teeth, settling back down into the chair in front my lawyer's desk. "How can this happen?" I feel my sister next to me, her silent "calm downs" reach me, but ultimately do no good. I can feel the panic of failure rise up like bile in my throat. The conference to schedule the hearing that might ultimately terminate the parental rights of Devon's biologicals was everything, and seeing her name on the court docket had nearly unhinged me.

"You know how the courts are, Carla," my lawyer says to me sooth-ingly. "One kid, one judge. But everything is going to be fine. We have our ducks in a row, and you've done your due diligence--this isn't like last time."

I cringe at the thought of "last time," last time when I was "just" my son's foster parent, with no rights, no support. I couldn't even appeal the decision that took him away. And he was right, if she took him away this time, there'd be nothing left of me. This would be so much worse than last time.

I clear both the memory and the negativity from my mind, lift and release my shoulder's in a heavy sigh, nod decisively. "Let's do this."

I follow my sister through the heavy swinging doors of the courtroom. At this point, I feel almost at home here. So much of our battle has been fought from these benches, and from the witness stand now standing empty before me. Surrenders, defeats, and victories tallied not so much by blood spilt, but papers signed. I can feel my confidence coming back a little. Looking around the thinly populated courtroom, I have no fear of running into the biologicals.

They never come.

For all her weeping and wailing, the woman who fought me for so long for claim to my child, had not once shown her face in the only arena in which she might prove she deserved him. Today, we are gathered, to terminate her rights once and for all.

"All rise," the bailiff says in the flat brown voice of nearly every bailiff I'd encountered. It had the peculiar quality of being both bored and watchful all at once. If was oddly comforting in this place that ate up so much of my time and money. Turning my head from the bailiff with a smile, I could feel it freeze on my face, then crack into a million pieces. A small *poof* escapes me as *all the air leaves my body.*

I finally see the judge for the first time.

Those bouncy brown curls, and carefully made up face, her very presence was like having ice water thrown down the middle of my naked back. This woman, this mother, this *officer of the court*, would forever be the woman who sent my baby to his biological mother - directly into the cycle of poverty and abuse.

Gripping the table to steady myself, I study this judge as she flounces her robe, and runs freshly manicured fingers through her hair. Does she really know who I am? Would she ever look me in my face and know the extent of what her decision had done to us? Her signature set every hardship, every indignity, every sacrifice we'd had to make into motion; it was her signature that ultimately brought us here before her today.

I wonder how her life had been these past eight years. Had her daughter watched everyone she loved try their best to ruin and corrupt everything good within her? Did she get a call letting her know that her child had attempted suicide, yet again, in response to the horrible things she'd experienced? Though I couldn't be certain, my hunch was no. No, this judge who indiscriminately impacted the lives of children and their families, no doubt slept soundly at night.

Court goes by in clips. As suspected, my son's birth parents are a no-show, although they were both served. Wayne was served while doing time in the county jail for a parole violation. Montaya was served in the parking lot of Auto Zone where she lived in her car. Due to the serious nature of the case, both were given court appointed lawyers. At one point the ex-husband was named in the original case many years ago, but he made it clear he wanted nothing to do with any of it.

With no one left to call, I make my way to the witness stand. Throughout the hearing, our *honorable* Judge had relied heavily upon law books with outdated statutes and I felt my hope slip away little by little. She seemed to have such little facility with the laws that could make or break our little family, and her previous lack of regard for my son's ultimate well-being, makes me feel bitter. That such important decisions could be placed in these hands further suggests to me that we aren't people, just numbers on papers.

Though my son's biological mother had been clean for a brief time upon his birth, this judge hadn't seen it necessary to ask for a mental competency check, a drug test, home visits, nothing. The same ignorance that took him away eight years ago would put him right back into a system which had already taken so much from him.

"What is your relationship to the child?" She asks me conversationally, as if the pages upon pages of paperwork, documents, and evidence, didn't point to the most obvious answer in the world.

"I'm his mother, I say it clearly, distinctly. "I've always been his mother. From the moment he was put into my arms, when he was taken away...I look at her, letting my words lean in, but she doesn't flinch. She either doesn't care, or she doesn't know. Neither would surprise me. "He's been my concern since I laid eyes on him," I finish a bit unsteady. I can tell from the look on my lawyer's face that I've said too much, but I can't help it. All the frustration I've felt since this entire ordeal began has a single origin, a single starting point. I can never fully blame his biological mom for the things she's done; she simply doesn't know any better. But this woman? To her, I have so much to say.

"And his birth mother, what type of connection would you say he has with her?" She continues her questions. I can feel the sweat beading around my hairline and I'm uncomfortable. I feel stifled by these questions and the whole thing is taking too long.

"He might have some good memories," I say without humor. "What child wouldn't love an adult who enforces nothing? He remembers a mother that was permissive, but angry. He remembers a mother that didn't give him a bedtime, but tried to run his father down in the street like a dog while he rode in the back seat terrified." Her eyes widen at this last bit of info. It's in his file, so I can tell she hasn't read it all, but I do feel a small sense of satisfaction. She should hear this.

"And his father," she asks without preamble, "what's the relationship like with him?"

"He idolizes his father," I don't see a reason to lie to her. "his father is a man that knows everything; from football to rap songs. He hangs on to every word he says. His father has taught him that 'bitches ain't shit, get them before they get you,' and a wealth of other life lessons." I can't help the bitterness that has crept into my voice. I know I should tread lightly here, and my sister will no doubt give me the business when we debrief, but I don't care. This woman makes me nervous, makes me mad, and I'm sick of being quiet about it.

After nearly 50 minutes on the stand, I'm released back to my now cold seat. I don't know what will happen, but I've said what I needed to say, and I find myself merely tired. The time and effort spent to get here, weighs heavily on me, and I just want it to be over. Please let it be over soon.

EPILOGUE

"Boys!" I call form the kitchen, really using my diaphragm to cut through the din of video games and what sounds like a herd of elephants upstairs. I crane my ear, and though it might be undetectable to the untrained ear, there is a brief cessation of noise that lets me know I'll soon have three hungry boys at my table, ready to eat.

I drink in the momentary silence with a smile and take the time to look through the sun-soaked kitchen window into my new backyard, and count my blessings.

My son's parents were ultimately found to be wholly unfit for the task of raising him, and as I had hoped, their rights had been terminated without fanfare. My brows slipped a little at this. Though they had been terrible parents, my son loves them, and hadn't seen them in nearly two years, nor was he ever likely to see them again. They would never see the sweet, patient boy he was growing to be. They would never see how hard he worked every day to override their programming, which was the same programming that changed them from victims to victimizers. His gentleness and perseverance, in light of all he'd been through, never ceased to amaze me.

Three pairs of feet clomped down the stairs, bringing with them noise, and joy, and a peace I thought I might never find.

Since the termination hearing, I'd made the decision to move. Though I was no longer afraid of the biologicals ability to wrest my son away from me, I couldn't really be sure how they might respond to the court order. Out of safety and a pressing need for a fresh start, I sold the house that held so many of our most terrible memories, and bought us a new one. My son and I had a new address, and with it, a new beginning.

I rustled together sandwiches, chips, and drinks from the fridge-a pro at this type of thing by now, and smiled at the easy banter between my son and his "play brothers." They were two boys brought to us by different circumstances, both a bit older, that we'd come to love, and who had come to love us.

I thought of the woman I used to be, and could barely find her in the woman I was today. A single mother, and more myself than I had ever been. I was proud of what we created.

Long before the termination hearing, I'd put the wheels of adoption into motion and one by one, things had clicked into place. The home visit had gone well, and my diligent record-keeping told the agency everything needed to be known about the home I created for my son. In this home, he was respected. In this home, he was cared for. In this home, he was loved, and most importantly, safe.

Sandwiches dispensed, I take my place at the table, we say our grace, and I wait patiently to disclose the contents of the letter clutched in my hand:

NOW THEREFORE, it is hereby ordered, adjudged, and decreed by the Court:

1. That from the date of entry of this Decree herein, the said minor is declared adopted for life by the petitioner and that said child shall henceforth be know by...

We had always shared love, and now we would share the same last name; a symbol of our forever bond as mother and son. He was always my son. Now it was legal.

Thank you, Lord.